DOOR
Birmingham Repertory Theatre

kalí
THEATRE COMPANY

C000049692

Birmingham Repertory Theatre company and Kali Theatre company present
The World Premiere of

Deadeye
by **Amber Lone**

First performed on 12 October 2006 at The Door, Birmingham Repertory Theatre

Following its run at The Door (Thu 12 – Sat 28 October), **Deadeye** plays at the following venues:

Fri 3 – Sat 4 November: Djanogly Theatre, Lakeside Arts Centre, Nottingham

Wed 8 – Thu 9 November: Contact, Manchester

Tue 14 – Sat 18 November: Soho Theatre, London

Birmingham Repertory Theatre
Centenary Square
Broad Street
Birmingham
B1 2EP
www.the-door.co.uk

Deadeye

by **Amber Lone**

Tariq **Shane Zaza**
Deema **Chetna Pandya**
Zainab **Sakuntala Ramanee**
Rafique **Madhav Sharma**
Jimmy **Pushpinder Chani**
Kerry **Beth Vyse**

Director **Janet Steel**
Designer **Matthew Wright**
Lighting Designer **Simon Bond**
Assistant Director **Sayan Kent**
Dialect Coach **Sarah Simmons**

Company Stage Manager **Andy Beardmore**
Assistant Stage Manager **Tabatha Williams**

Biographies

Shane Zaza
Tariq

Shane trained at the National Youth Theatre. **Theatre** includes: *Furnace Four* (Soho Theatre); *Billy Liar* (Liverpool Playhouse); *Mercury Fur* (Paines Plough); *Minutes Pass* (Polka Theatre); *George's Marvellous Medicine* (Bolton Octagon); *The Long Way Home* (New Perspectives); *East Is East* (New Vic Theatre); *Master And Margarita*, *Kes*, *Dot Com*, *The Arbitrary Adventures Of An Accidental Terrorist* and *Nicholas Nickleby* (NYT/Lyric Hammersmith). **Television** includes: *Murphy's Law*, *Dalziel & Pascoe*, *Waterloo Road*, *Doctors*, *Messiah*, *Casualty*, *Watch Over Me* and *The Bill*. **Film** includes: *The Da Vinci Code*. **Radio** includes: *Orwell's Babies*.

Chetna Pandya
Deema

Chetna trained at Mountview. **Theatre** credits include: *Coram Boy* (National Theatre); *Lucky Stiff* (New Wimbledon Theatre); *Hurting Too Much*, *Rubik's Cube*, *Shame On You*, *Krishna's Tea Party* and *Zameen* (Kali Theatre Company); *Romeo & Juliet* (Changeling Theatre Co); *Best Little Warehouse In Texas* (Centre Stage/Millfield Theatre) and *In Our Time* (London Palladium). **Television** credits include: *Broken News*, *The Worst Week Of My Life*, *Green Wing*, *The Message*, *New Tricks* and *Doctors*. **Radio** includes: *Bitter Fruits Of Palestine*.

Sakuntala Ramanee
Zainab

Theatre credits include: *Tales From The Firozsha Baag* (National Theatre Studio); *Trust* (National Theatre Studio); *Camille* (Lyric Hammersmith); *The Maharajah's Daughter* (Oval House); *Maa* (Royal Court); *India Song* (Theatre Clwyd); *House Of The Sun* (Theatre Royal, Stratford); *Around The World In Eight Days* (Southampton); *The Mysteries* (Belgrade Coventry) and *Amongst Barbarians* (Royal Exchange). **Television and film** credits include: *Dalziel And Pascoe*, *Emmerdale*, *If I Had You*, *Wish Baby*, *The Brief*, *The Bill*, *Where The Heart Is*, *Murder In Suburbia*, *Trust Me I'm A Prime Minister*, *Hustle*, *Behind Closed Doors*, *24 Seven*, *Bollywood Queen*, *Indian Summer*, *The Butterfly Effect*, *Murder In Mind*, *Doctors*, *Holby City*, *The Safe House*, *Big Kids*, *Grange Hill*, *Out Of Sight*, *Casualty*, *EastEnders* and *Stone Cold*. **Radio** credits include: numerous radio dramas for Pam Frazer Soloman, Martin Jenkins, Alison Hindell, Kristine Landon-Smith and Vanessa Whitburn.

Madhav Sharma
Rafique

It all began with touring Shakespeare in India, Singapore, Malaysia, Sarawak, Brunei, N. Borneo and Hong Kong, followed by a scholarship to RADA and a career of some four decades so far. **Theatre** includes: *Behzti* (Birmingham Repertory Theatre); *Calcutta Kosher*, *Worlds Apart*, *House Of The Sun* (Theatre Royal Stratford East); *The King And I* (West End tour); *The Accused* (Haymarket and tour); *Last Dance At Dum Dum* (New

Ambassadors/tour); *Crazy Horse* (Bristol New Vic/tour); *Not Just An Asian Babe* (Watermans); *Indian Ink* (Aldwych); *High Diplomacy* (Westminster); *Untold Secret Of Aspi* (Cockpit); *Thérèse Raquin* (Nottingham Playhouse); *Twelfth Night* (Dundee Theatre Royal); *Romeo And Juliet* (Shaw/Edinburgh Festival/USA); *The Importance Of Being Neutral* (ICA); *Fiddler On The Roof* (tour); *Blithe Spirit* (Birmingham Repertory Theatre); and the title role in *Hamlet* (The Howff). **Recent television** includes: *Casualty*, *Reverse Psychology*, *Coronation Street*, *Grease Monkeys*, *Doctors And Nurses*, *Innocents*, *Dalziel And Pascoe*, *Holby City*, *Dream Team*, *Amongst Barbarians*, *Trial And Retribution*, *McCallum*, *Fighting Back*, *Inspector Alleyn*, *The Rector's Wife*, *Tygo Road*, *Cardiac Arrest*, *Shalom Salaam*, *Black And Blue*, *Medics*, *Boon*, *This Office Life*, *The Bill*, *South Of The Border*, *King And Castle*, *Tandoori Nights*, *Old Men At The Zoo*, *Maybury*, *Minder*, *Target*, *The Road To 1984*, *Blunt Instrument*, *Cold Warrior*, *Sarah*, *Looking For Clancy*, *The Regiment*, *Imperial Palace*, *Adam Smith*, *The Brahmin Widow*, *First Lady*, *Moonbase 3*, *Doctor Who*, *Anything But The Woods*, *Rogue's Rock*, *The Moonstone* and *Uncle Tulip*. Madhav also directs in the theatre, and has appeared in numerous films, including *Entrapment* and *East Is East* and many radio plays, most recently *A House For Mr Biswas*.

Pushpinder Chani
Jimmy

Pushpinder trained at Carlton Television Workshops and Birmingham Theatre School. **Theatre** includes: *Paper Thin* (Kali Theatre); *What We Did To Weinstein* (Menier Chocolate Factory); *Twelfth Night* (The Stage Works); *Midnight's Children* (Royal Shakespeare Company); *Baiju Bawra* (Theatre Royal Statford East); *14 Songs, 2 Weddings And A Funeral* (Tamasha Theatre Company); *Made In India* (Leicester Haymarket), and *Transmissions* Festival (Birmingham Repertory Theatre). He has worked extensively for **Theatre In Education** companies, including Women And Theatre, Catalyst, Language Alive and Speakeasy Theatre. **Television** includes: *Fair City*, *Life Isn't All Ha Ha Hee Hee*, *Doctors* and *Casualty*. **Radio** includes: Currently in *Silver Street*, *Behind Closed Doors*, *A Minus* and *Ties*. **Films** include: *Almost Adult* and *Cross My Heart* and *Anita And Me*.

Beth Vyse
Kerry

Beth trained at Rose Bruford. **Theatre** credits include: *Silence* (Arcola Theatre); *Beauty And The Beast* (Royal Shakespeare Company); *Tamer Tamed* (RSC/ West End); *Birdsong* (RSC); *A Day In Dull Armour* (RSC, The Other Place); *The Taming Of The Shrew* (RSC/ West End); *Measure For Measure* (RSC) and *Mooney And His Caravans* (Greenwich). **Television** credits include: *My Family* and *Spooks*. **Film** credits include: *Action* (RSC Film Festival). **Radio** credits include: *Doctor Who* and *Culture Shock*.

Amber Lone
Writer

Amber Lone, originally from Birmingham, studied English & History at York University before settling in south London where she worked as a refuge and resettlement worker for a variety of projects, providing support to Asian women. Amber's first full-length play *Paradise*, about a young boy's journey towards radical Islam, was produced at Birmingham Repertory

Theatre in 2003. She was selected as one of six writers for Soho Theatre's Writers Attachment Programme in 2004–05, and her other writing credits include a short play for M6 Theatre Company. Amber is currently writing a full-length play for Theatre Centre and is a member of the Red Room Writers' Group. For radio, Amber's first play *Ties* was broadcast on Radio 4 in March 2004, and she has also written numerous episodes of *Westway* (BBC World Service). Amber is represented by Micheline Steinberg Associates (info@ steinplays.com).

Janet Steel
Director

Janet has been Artistic Director of Kali Theatre Company since 2003. She began her career as an actress, her **theatre** work includes: *Cinders* and *A Colder Climate* (Royal Court Theatre); *Blood Wedding* (Half Moon); *Romeo And Juliet* (Sherman Theatre & Albany Empire) and *Oedipus Rex* (Tara Arts). **Television** credits include: *An English Christmas*, *The Bride*, *Gems*, *The Refuge* and *Shalom Salaam*. Janet began directing in 1988 as assistant to Tessa Schneideman at Loose Change Theatre, producing UK premières at BAC by Spanish authors, where she directed her first full-length piece, *White Biting Dog*. **Directing** includes: *Behzti* (Birmingham Repertory Theatre); *April In Paris, Bretevski Street, A Hard Rain* and *Top Girls* (Northampton Royal Theatre); *Exodus (*Millennium Mysteries at Coventry Belgrade); Brecht's *Antigone, The Mother, Orpheus Descending, An Ideal Husband, Romeo & Juliet, The Knockey* and *Serious Money* (Rose Bruford College). **For Kali Theatre**: *Sock 'Em With Honey* by Bapsi Sidhwa, *Calcutta Kosher* by Shelley Silas, *Chaos* and *Paper Thin* by Azma Dar.

Matthew Wright
Designer

Matthew trained at the Glasgow School of Art in Textile Design. Designs for **theatre** include: *In Praise Of Love* (Chichester Festival Theatre); *Speaking Like Magpies* (Royal Shakespeare Company); *One Under* (Tricycle); *Clouds* (UK tour); *Paper Thin* (Kali Theatre); *Us And Them, The Dead Eye Boy* (Hampstead); *The Green Man, Presence, Royal Supreme, Blood Red Saffron Yellow, Musik, The Imposter* (Theatre Royal Plymouth); *Summer Lightning, Amy's View* (Salisbury), *Arcadia* (Theatre Royal Northampton); *Dancing At Lughnasa, Four Nights In Knaresborough, All That Trouble We Had* (New Victoria Theatre, Stoke); *Private Lives, Charley's Aunt* (Northcott Exeter); *Larkin With Women* (West Yorkshire Playhouse); *The Deep Blue Sea, Neville's Island, A Taste Of Honey* (Watford Palace); *Confusions, Habeus Corpus* (Salisbury); *Summer Lightning* (Salisbury & Theatre Royal Bath); *End Of The Affair* (Salisbury/Bridewell); *Our Country's Good* (Edinburgh Lyceum); *Hamlet* (RNT Education); *Woman In Mind* (Theatre Royal York); *Twelfth Night, Hamlet* (OSC); *Romeo And Juliet* (Greenwich) and *Pow!* (Paines Plough). Other **designs for Birmingham Repertory Theatre** include: *Katherine Desouza, Behzti, Getting To The Foot Of The Mountain, Swamp City, Bells* and *Chaos* (Kali Theatre Company), and *On The Ceiling,* which also played in the West End. **Opera** credits include *Ii Pomo D'oro* (Batignano Opera Festival) and *Don Pasquale* (Scottish Opera Go Round). Matthew also designed the costumes for *Seriously Funny* for Channel Four Television.

Simon Bond
Lighting Designer

Simon Bond works at the Birmingham Repertory Theatre as a lighting technician. **Recent designs** include

Katherine Desouza, *The Bolt Hole*, *The Santaland Diaries* and *Season's Greetings To All Our Friends And Family*. He first experienced touring theatre last year with the Pentabus production of *Strawberry Fields* and has just worked with them again on *White Open Spaces* which, after a successful stint at the Edinburgh Fringe festival, is now transferring to the Soho Theatre in London.

Sayan Kent
Assistant Director

Sayan was born in London and trained as an actress at Rose Bruford. **Directing** includes several staged readings for Kali Theatre Company and Watermans, and assistant director on *Good Golly Miss Molly* (Arts Theatre). She also works as an actor, composer, writer and dramaturg. **Writing** includes *Housewife's Choice* (LBC radio); and co-writing musical adaptations of *Silas Marner* (Belgrade, Coventry); *The Good Companions* (New Vic, Stoke); and three pantomimes. **Composing** includes *Chaos*, *Sock'em With Honey* and *Calcutta Kosher* (Kali Theatre), *Hound Of The Baskervilles* (Paul Farrah Productions), *The Phantom Sausage* (Wolsey, Ipswich), *The Turn Of The Screw*, *Limestone Cowboy* and *Cinderella* (Coventry Belgrade); *Truckers* (Harrogate); *A Hard Rain* (Northampton); *Country* (New Vic Stoke); *Dinosaur Dreams* (Unicorn); *Hot Doris The Musical* (Oval House); *Factory Follies* (Croydon Warehouse); *72 Days* and *Bloody Elektra* (Oval House and Albany Empire); *Good Companions*, *Silas Marner*, *Mother Goose*, *Dick Whittington* and *Aladdin*. She was, for four years, songwriter/performer with The Hot Doris Band. **Acting** includes leading roles in many regional theatres and her **TV/Film** work includes: *Coronation Street*, *EastEnders*, *Moveable Feasts*, *The Bill*, *The Big Battalions*, *The Paradise Club*, *Young Soul Rebels* and recently *Doctors*.

Andy Beardmore
Company Stage Manager

Andy is pleased to be returning to Kali for *Deadeye*. Previous to this Andy was stage managing *Lies have Been Told* (Trafalgar Studios; Pleasance, Edinburgh), Production Manager for *The Gaydar Diaries* (Brighton; Pleasance, London; Edinburgh), Company Stage Manager for *Paper Thin* (Kali Theatre) and *The Ratcatcher Of Hamelin* (BAC), Stage Manager for *'Tis Pity She's A Whore* (Jermyn Street). Andy Studied at Rose Bruford College where he gained a BA (hons) in Stage Management. Alongside his training Andy co-founded and produced for Sulis Productions, for whom he has produced and stage managed various UK and International tours including their tour to the Adelaide Fringe festival 2004.

Tabatha Williams
Assistant Stage Manager

Tabatha has recently moved to London from America to further develop her career in theatre. Tabatha has a background in acting, directing, and stage management. Her previous **American stage management** credits include: *Children Of A Lesser God* and *The Crucible* (Gilbreath Theatre); *Keely And Du* (Patchwork Theatre); *Our Town* (VA Memorial Theatre) and *Happy Days* (Vanguard Theatre Company). Tabatha began her experience in London working for Kali Theatre Company on *Paper Thin* this past winter. Tabatha's **London stage management** credits also include *Wild Fruit* and *Faithless Bitches* (Oval House Theatre); and most recently *Ella, Meet Marilyn*, which performed at the Rosemary Branch and the Edinburgh Fringe Festival. Tabatha is very excited to be working with Kali again and feels that it was an excellent way to start and end a beautiful first year in the British theatre scene.

ᴛʜᴇ**DOOR**
Birmingham Repertory Theatre

Birmingham Repertory Theatre is one of Britain's leading national producing theatre companies. Under the recent Artistic Direction of Jonathan Church, The REP has enjoyed great success with a busy and exciting programme. Rachel Kavanaugh has recently taken over the role of Artistic Director, and we look forward to announcing her first season of work later this year

The REP's productions regularly transfer to London, tour nationally and internationally. Recent and tours have included *Glorious!*, *The Birthday Party*, *The Witches*, *Through The Woods*, *Of Mice And Men*, *A Doll's House*, *The Crucible*, *Celestina*, *Hamlet*, *The Ugly Eagle*, *The Old Masters*, *The Snowman*, *The Gift*, *Behsharam (Shameless)* and *The Ramayana*.

The commissioning and production of new work lies at the core of The REP's programme. The Door was established eight years ago as a theatre dedicated to the production and presentation of new writing. In this time, it has given world premières to new plays from a new generation of British playwrights including Abi Morgan, Moira Buffini, Bryony Lavery, Crispin Whittell, Paul Lucas, Gurpreet Kaur Bhatti, Sarah Woods, Roy Williams, Kaite O'Reilly, Ray Grewal, Jess Walters, Jonathan Harvey, Tamsin Oglesby, Sarah Daniels, Shan Khan, Arzhang Pezhman and Nick Stafford. The REP itself received The Peggy Ramsey Award for New Writing, enabling us to develop and commission more new plays for the future.

The Door aims to provide a distinct alternative to the work seen in the Main House; a space where new voices and contemporary stories can be heard, and to create new audiences for the work of the company. The Door is also a place to explore new ideas and different approaches to making theatre, and to develop new plays and support emerging companies. It also emphasises work for and by young people, through *Transmissions*, our *First Stages* childrens' theatre programme, and the strong emphasis on work by living writers within *The Young REP*, our youth theatre initiative.

Transmissions – our young writers' programme – gives writers ages 12 to 25 the opportunity to work with professional playwrights to develop initial ideas into complete scripts. This year our young writers will be collaborating with our youth theatre, *The Young REP*, to produce a set of site-specific plays in the historic Old Rep theatre on Station Street. These plays will be performed during GENERATION, a festival of new work for and by young people, to be held at The REP in Spring 2007. *Transmissions* also has an outreach programme supported by the Paul Hamlyn Foundation, with schools from across the region participating.

phf THE PAUL HAMLYN FOUNDATION

"Transmissions hurtled into its second week, blazing with energy and delivering some of the most provocative and original new work to be seen anywhere in the city" Birmingham Post

"A rich and extraordinary assortment of tomorrow's talent" Evening Mail

"It is a brilliant enterprise" Birmingham Post

For more information about the work of The Door or about our work with new writers, please contact Ben Payne or Caroline Jester on 0121 245 2000. If you are a writer and want more information about how to apply for one of our schemes, please send your contact details to literary@birmingham-rep.co.uk or call 0121 245 2045, and we will contact you when we advertise for submissions.

Birmingham City Council

Artistic Director Rachel Kavanaugh
Executive Director Stuart Rogers
Associate Director (Literary) Ben Payne

European Community
European Regional Development Fund

Book online at www.the-door.co.uk
Birmingham Repertory Theatre is a registered charity, number 223660

ARTS COUNCIL ENGLAND

kali
THEATRE COMPANY

Kali seeks out strong individual Asian women writers who challenge our perceptions through original and thought provoking theatre. The company has established a reputation for presenting work that takes audiences on unpredictable journeys that entertain, excite and inspire.

Since its inception in 1990, Kali's connections within the Asian community have made it a natural home for women who are seeking new ways to express and explore the issues and human interest stories of the Diaspora.

Kali aims to present the distinct perspective and experience of Asian women to people from all backgrounds and to celebrate that richness and diversity. No idea is too small, no statement too large. We actively encourage our writers and audience to reinvent and reshape the theatrical agenda.

Deadeye will be the centrepiece of **Asian Women *Talk Back***, Kali's festival of new writing by Asian Women at Soho Theatre in London, 14 – 25 November 2006, presented with support from Bloomberg.

See **www.kalitheatre.co.uk** for further details

Artistic Director Janet Steel
Associate Director Shabina Aslam
Administrator Simeilia Hodge-Dallaway
Consultant General Manager Christopher Corner

Kali was founded by **Rukhsana Ahmad** and **Rita Wolf**.

Kali Theatre Company Ltd
18 Rupert Street
London W1D 6DE
020 7494 9100
info@kalitheatre.co.uk

Funded by

Supported by:

Bloomberg
and the Peggy Ramsay Foundation

DEADEYE

First published in 2006 by Oberon Books Ltd.
521 Caledonian Road, London N7 9RH
Tel: 020 7607 3637 / Fax: 020 7607 3629
e-mail: info@oberonbooks.com
www.oberonbooks.com

A catalogue record for this book is available from the British Library.

ISBN: 1 84002 707 X / 978-1-84002-707-5

Cover image: Fluid

Printed in Great Britain by Antony Rowe Ltd, Chippenham.

Characters

TARIQ

DEEMA

ZAINAB

RAFIQUE

JIMMY

KERRY

*My deepest thanks to Carl Miller, Ben Payne, all at Kali
theatre and to my many friends and loved ones who have
been a constant source of encouragement and support.*

*For the magnificent eight: Emile, Deon, Surraya, Raisa,
Rameez, Aslam, Rehan and Kassim*

Act One

Indoors. Back room of the Chaudhrys' terraced house on an inner-city street, West Midlands. Peeling painted wallpaper and general disrepair. It is the middle of the night / early hours of the morning. DEEMA is sleeping, a shadow in a blanket on a large old sofa, which is covered with home-made floral cotton cover. Very little furniture in the room aside from a small table. A few books, French language aids and a large address book lie closed on the table alongside a couple of the day's papers. Television is flickering and at very low volume.

TARIQ enters, carrying a white plastic bag, quite full. He puts the bag down very slowly. He starts to rummage through things in the room. He tiptoes about, checking clothes and snooping. He sees DEEMA's handbag / college bag and tries to pull it away from her, as stealthily and as slowly as possible, but he ends up bending face-forward on to DEEMA who screams and wakes up.

TARIQ: Shush… It's me.

    TARIQ switches the lights on.

DEEMA: Fucken hell…you scared the shit out of…

TARIQ: Sos man.

DEEMA: What are you doin' you idiot? What time is it?

TARIQ: Ten past four…

DEEMA: (*Loudly.*) I was sleeping.

TARIQ: Shush…you don't have to scream man… What you doin' downstairs then? Watching telly?

DEEMA: Does it look like it? I was working. You don't just…

TARIQ: College work? Did you get it done?

DEEMA: …walk in on people in the middle of… I've gotta be up in a few hours.

TARIQ: You should go to bed man.

DEEMA: I was on my way.

TARIQ: You need a proper sleep when you're studyin'.

DEEMA: What were you up to?

TARIQ: Just checking in.

DEEMA: After four weeks…just checking in? You expect me to
    believe that?

TARIQ: It's true. Look, I was at a mate's… It ain't my fault
    you've got work to do… What is it…? Need any help?

DEEMA: Just some job applications…no, it's nothing… I don't
    need any… You were looking for something.

TARIQ: I wasn't.

DEEMA: You were in my bag.

TARIQ: No, I wasn't… Did you see…everything was fallin' out
    of it.

*TARIQ picks the bag up and passes it to her and she puts it down
a little closer*

What? D'you think I was gonna nick something from ya?
(*Beat.*) You did! You don't give me a chance man. Who
d'you think I am?

DEEMA: I didn't say.

TARIQ: You din't have to… If I want anything I'll ask ya
    straight alright?

DEEMA: I ain't got any money.

TARIQ: Hold on Deema…

DEEMA: I haven't.

TARIQ: Just listen a sec.

DEEMA: Where's your money?

TARIQ: I owed someone…but I only need a couple o' quid.

DEEMA: If you want fags, they're in my bag… I know there are. (*DEEMA rummages in the bag and pulls out an empty packet, which TARIQ emptied earlier.*) There were a couple in there.

TARIQ: Probably forgot you smoked 'em.

DEEMA: I didn't forget I fucken smoked 'em alright…

DEEMA throws the bag down.

TARIQ: Oy.

DEEMA: What?

TARIQ: Fucken this and fucken that! You wanna relax man, you'll give yerself a heart attack. I don't need fags. Just calm down will ya? D'you want a cup o' tea? I'll make you a cup of tea…

DEEMA: No, I don't.

TARIQ: Sos sis, sos man.

DEEMA: All I've got is my bus fare.

TARIQ: You wanna get some balance Deem…you're overdoing it…studyin' French and graftin' an all… Your brain'll overload man.

DEEMA: It's a part-time job in Habitat Tariq…and I like languages.

TARIQ: Just need a sub… D'you reckon mum / or dad…

DEEMA: Mum or dad? They ain't got any money for you.

TARIQ: Only a couple o' quid.

DEEMA: I don't have it…that's the truth… Have to be up soon Tariq.

TARIQ: I wouldn't ask but I've got somethin' on tomorra… (*Beat.*) Kind of…well…there's this guy, mate of Jimmy's… uptown in this warehouse, says I might be able to get a job loadin' parcels…says to come an' talk to him. It's just to get the bus there and back. I'll give it ya back. I'll come here straight after.

DEEMA: You get a giro.

TARIQ: Yeah I know that but it's due the day after… But I'll have a word…the guy's safe…he'll let me cash it a day early.

DEEMA: Tariq…

TARIQ: Told ya. I promise man. Kusmeh. Tomorra I'll cash my cheque and come to yours. You can come with me if you don't believe me… Or take it…you cash it and take yer money.

DEEMA: I'm not begging some post office guy for a favour.

TARIQ: Then tell me when you're back and I'll be here waiting.

DEEMA pulls out a fiver and hands it over.

Thanks sis… What time you back from college?

DEEMA: Where you goin'?

TARIQ: I'll stop at Jimmy's…it's nearer to town.

DEEMA: You gonna tell mum and dad where you've been?

TARIQ: Don't worry.

DEEMA: Keep the noise down…I don't want them waking up.

TARIQ: Thanks sis man. You'll see…once I start earning, you won't have to worry about me…I can lend you money.

DEEMA: Just go.

TARIQ: I mean it.

DEEMA: Yeah, yeah alright.

DEEMA lies back down on the sofa.

TARIQ: (*Whispering.*) Deem.

DEEMA: What?

TARIQ: Thanks alright?

DEEMA: Yeah.

TARIQ: I'll come down okay.

DEEMA: F…

TARIQ: Okay, okay.

TARIQ tiptoes out but ends up tripping over and falling.

DEEMA: For fuck's sake!

DEEMA pulls the blanket over her head and curls up.

Blackout.

SCENE TWO

The next day. Garden of the same house. Noon. A warm, late summer day. Bright but a few clouds hovering nearby. Brick-built tandoor oven upstage on one side. A pile of old newspapers on the ground near the tandoor. A satchel-type book bag lies on a chair, carrying a file and books. A mismatch of plants: chick-peas, runner beans, coriander in a section of the garden bricked off. A couple of stone pots and a few old buckets, also serving as plant pots, with plants growing in them. The soil is damp as ZAINAB has just finished watering the plants. ZAINAB is cleaning dahl on a tray, sitting one side of tandoor. DEEMA is gathering branches for the tandoor from a pile at the other end of the garden offstage. The opposite side to the tandoor is the back gate / door which leads onto the street. Sitting close to the gate are several large cardboard boxes full of books. ZAINAB steps down from her stoup, walks over to the boxes, pokes inside, looks down the alley-way and returns to her stoup. DEEMA shouts to her mother.

DEEMA: It's gonna rain.

ZAINAB: It won't.

DEEMA enters carrying a bundle of branches in both arms, looking a little worn and irritated.

That's all you found? So many branches and you bring twigs?

DEEMA: These are the dry ones umee… (*DEEMA drops the branches and goes over to the bag and starts to order its contents neatly.*) It's gonna rain again.

ZAINAB: It won't rain.

Enter RAFIQUE from the back gate. He is dressed in an ill-matched and dated jacket-trousers combo – seventies throwback – and a worn, tieless shirt. He is half-dragging, half-carrying a large box. As he walks into the garden his legs seem to buckle under the weight. ZAINAB runs over and grabs the box as he almost falls.

Get out of the way.

RAFIQUE: Stand back.

ZAINAB: Please…before I am made a widow.

RAFIQUE brushes back his hair and sits down, breathless, clearly not up to lifting, as ZAINAB disappears down the alley-way. As she goes, RAFIQUE pulls a brochure out of the left-hand pocket of his old suit jacket. He calls DEEMA almost surreptitiously and she looks at him. He taps the brochure proudly.

DEEMA: Yeah, I know.

RAFIQUE: But look, you haven't seen it? (*Walking towards DEEMA, he steps into the plants unknowingly.*) Look…look at it…go on…read it…read it.

DEEMA: Dad.

RAFIQUE: Ey…ey… You can't cook now. I'm going out.

ZAINAB: So go after.

RAFIQUE: No time, no time…Malik is coming to pick me up.

DEEMA: You can't expect her to wait.

RAFIQUE: Who said she had to wait? Chall, I'll eat when I get back.

ZAINAB: We weren't going to starve ourselves for you.

RAFIQUE: What's food? I can eat whenever I want. This…this is worth going hungry for see?

ZAINAB sees the dishevelled plants and soil on RAFIQUE's shoe.

ZAINAB: Hai Mai! Will you look where you're going?

RAFIQUE: Meh keh keethaa? [What did I do?]

ZAINAB: (*Pushes him away from the plants.*) You've broken my bootey… [plants] They just started growing.

RAFIQUE: Okay poothar, [child] now look…see this one.

RAFIQUE ignores ZAINAB and beckons his daughter. She grudgingly comes towards him as ZAINAB pushes him away and starts clearing the mess.

Read it…go on…so your mother can hear.

DEEMA: She's busy.

RAFIQUE: Just for a minute.

DEEMA takes brochure.

DEEMA: 'Magnificent country estate set in twenty acres of land, surrounded by protected woodland, attached stables with planning permission to convert. Nearest town, Chester…nineteen miles. Manchester airport…one hour.'

RAFIQUE: Zaburdast [marvellous] huh?

DEEMA: How much?

RAFIQUE: You won't believe it… See there.

DEEMA: What?

RAFIQUE: See?

ZAINAB: Deema. Go wake your brother.

DEEMA: I'm doing something. 'Offers invited in the region of 1.9 million pounds…'

ZAINAB: Tell him come eat his roti.

RAFIQUE: What did I say? Giving it away / isn't it?

DEEMA: To millionaires I suppose.

RAFIQUE: And can people like us not be millionaires one day?

ZAINAB: Tell him stop sleeping.

DEEMA: Think about it dad…you have to live within your means…you're talking about buying…

RAFIQUE: Who is buying? I'm just looking… Go get / Tariq, Deema.

ZAINAB: Go have a look / will you?

DEEMA: / He isn't sleeping.

ZAINAB is gathering up the hose she was using to water the plants and which has been lying on the ground.

ZAINAB: I heard him last night.

DEEMA: It was me…doing an essay.

ZAINAB: I heard him talking.

DEEMA: I fell asleep with the telly on.

RAFIQUE: Make and save for him.

ZAINAB: He was going upstairs.

DEEMA: It was the telly. Umee…you have to stop worrying.

RAFIQUE: What do I do? Throw him away?

ZAINAB: How do I do that? How do I stop worrying?

RAFIQUE: He is not thinking of you. He is not caring about us.

ZAINAB: So long I have not seen his face.

DEEMA: Ha hasn't been home mom. What do you want me to say?

Beat.

RAFIQUE: Leave that matter…just see. What a thing to look at.

ZAINAB: Looking all your life.

RAFIQUE: This country…in parts it's very beautiful too… Yes…you have to search carefully for the gems and bright, warm days with such welcoming skies must never be ignored…they should be appreciated…savoured. This is a day to wonder at the beauty of things such as Chester House.

DEEMA: It's gonna pour down in a minute.

RAFIQUE: A few clouds that's all… 'Agar Firdaus bar roowai zumeeyast, Humaiyast thau, humaiyast thau, humaiyast thau.' 'If there is a paradise on earth…it is this…it is this, it is this…' (*Looking at brochure.*) Bright sunshine…green fields…like back home. You can live like a rajah in a place like this…like Nehru at the height of Congress… He and Mountbatten's wife had a fine dausthee did you know?

DEEMA: But dad…

RAFIQUE: Eh…the Queen would not like that eh…? Nehru and Mountbatten's wife?

DEEMA: I don't suppose… Look dad.

RAFIQUE: I know, I know but imagine Deema…waking up each morning to fresh food and a beautiful land…your land…master of your own kingdom. You tell me…what could beat such a feeling?

DEEMA: You're just torturing yourself.

ZAINAB: Not himself.

RAFIQUE: No poothar…not torture.

DEEMA: But if you can't live in this, this Chester place…what's the point?

RAFIQUE: Just a visit…take a walk, that's all… Want to come?

DEEMA: I'm busy. Take mum.

ZAINAB: I'm making dahl for the rajah.

RAFIQUE: See…look. Your rajah has a plan. He will show you what is possible with perseverance…hard work… determination.

DEEMA: It's eighty miles away and you don't have a car.

RAFIQUE: Foolish girl…Malik is there. If your brother had a brain, he would have a licence… If he did…maybe by now we would be there already…fishing by the lake. A father needs the backing of his sons.

DEEMA: What about me?

RAFIQUE: But I have my own two legs. They will carry me further than any hopes I have for him.

DEEMA grabs a book and looks inside.

DEEMA: This stuff is old dad…published in 1980.

RAFIQUE: That is very young poothar…a few years so? Did Malik phone?

ZAINAB: He can't.

RAFIQUE: Where is the book with the numbers? I'll call him… Why don't you come with me? I shall be Akbar, taking my Noor-Jehan for a sweetheart's stroll…my Mahal will equal his… What do you say dear wife?

ZAINAB: I'm busy. Deema bring the aataa [flour] and the tea-towels.

DEEMA moves and exits with ZAINAB's words following her.

But first bring me a glass of water…no, tea…my tea…make it strong achaa… [okay] My head is hurting and my throat is dry.

As DEEMA goes, ZAINAB speaks. DEEMA stands out of sight and listens..

There was a visit… Mr Dickson.

RAFIQUE: So?

ZAINAB: He said he must speak to you…urgent.

RAFIQUE: What is there to eat?

ZAINAB: Saag… If I had some money I could buy meat.

RAFIQUE: I'll get meat tomorrow.

ZAINAB: He said you didn't call him. He wants money.

RAFIQUE: All bank managers want money…their job is to steal your money.

ZAINAB: What if we have to leave?

RAFIQUE: You know the truly great thing about being here?

ZAINAB: There is no place for normal things.

RAFIQUE: After the knock down, after the kick, they still allow you to try your chance, to walk your path. Yes, you may fail, but that is no reason to quit. They say welcome, try your luck. Work hard, don't give up. I will never give up. God is on my side. He has never let me down. He tells me I have two hands and two feet. I have a mind and I may work wonders with it.

ZAINAB: You must call him.

RAFIQUE: We won't have to leave.

ZAINAB: Maybe Khan Sahib has some work in the warehouse?

RAFIQUE: Why waste time building another's empire? You have no imagination.

ZAINAB: How could I?

JIMMY enters carrying a large box.

JIMMY: Where d'you wan' it?

RAFIQUE: Just anywhere is fine poothar.

JIMMY goes to drop it in the centre of the garden.

ZAINAB: Not anywhere… Salaam Jamil.

JIMMY: Salaam aunty…my arms are killin' me.

ZAINAB directs him to the corner with the other boxes. He struggles.

ZAINAB: Just here is okay.

ZAINAB helps JIMMY lower the box and place it on the ground.

JIMMY: I'll be heading off then uncle.

RAFIQUE: Already…not before eating poothar.

JIMMY: I'm not hungry.

RAFIQUE: But tell us. Buying another shop your father tells me. Did you hear Zainab?

ZAINAB: Very good. Mubarak [congratulations] to you.

JIMMY: Not just yet aunty. But maybe in the future.

RAFIQUE: Why not? Push on my son! Push on and you shall be rewarded. By God you shall! Tell me. What are your plans?

RAFIQUE pats JIMMY on the shoulders.

JIMMY: Maybe a chain of supermarkets you know… 'Mahmood and Sons'.

RAFIQUE: Of course yaar…but your plans today?

JIMMY: Erm…

RAFIQUE: Fancy a drive? It is a gift of an afternoon. We shouldn't waste it.

JIMMY: Well.

RAFIQUE: There is a wonderful thing which must be seen. You know how it is. We must have our distractions from this pain-filled world.

ZAINAB: That would be nice.

RAFIQUE: Kyoo nahin? [Why not?] So what do you say son? It's not far…just down the road.

JIMMY: Course…where?

RAFIQUE: A little way from Manchester.

JIMMY: Manchester? That ain't down the road.

RAFIQUE: Waah? That is not far. You youngsters have no sense of adventure… Sometimes…even businessmen take holeeday.

JIMMY: No really. I have to go…

RAFIQUE: Okay okay but poothar…

RAFIQUE pats JIMMY on the shoulder.

To do well at work we must also remember to find ways to take our rest or get a help…somebody to share the load…

They exit as DEEMA reappears.

DEEMA: Can I go now umee?

ZAINAB: Where?

DEEMA: Careers fair at college.

ZAINAB: Where is the aataa?

DEEMA: Dunno…

ZAINAB: I told you do the aataa…

DEEMA: Sorry mum…

ZAINAB: Last night, after washing up, I told you.

DEEMA: I didn't hear you.

ZAINAB: Where is your mind?

DEEMA: Told you…I've got a college do.

RAFIQUE re-enters, impatient and anxious.

RAFIQUE: Who has broken the phone?

DEEMA: (*To ZAINAB.*) What's the matter… I'll do the aataa now.

RAFIQUE: It's not working…the phone is broken…Zainab?

ZAINAB: Not broken.

RAFIQUE: I can't dial out…I'm saying.

ZAINAB grabs a bill from a pile of papers on the tandoor and hands it to RAFIQUE.

Never mind…I'll walk to Malik's.

RAFIQUE takes the bill and walks out of the alley-way.

DEEMA: I know umee.

ZAINAB: Keh? There is nothing to know.

DEEMA: I know about the house. I know we've been cut off.

ZAINAB: He will make right.

DEEMA: Shall I do the aataa before I go?

ZAINAB: Leave it. There is enough for one.

ZAINAB exits into the kitchen. DEEMA watches her.

SCENE THREE

A week later. A room in a council flat. Late afternoon. Starkly lit. Ripped, mock leather sofa and wooden table with cotton covers thrown onto the furniture. A tiny metallic ashtray on the floor and a flashy television in the corner. TARIQ is smoking a cigarette and getting increasingly agitated, standing up, sitting down, pacing the room and banging on the wall behind him. He wears beaten trainers, loose, grubby tracksuit bottoms and a baggy, black jumper. His face is gaunt.

TARIQ: Come on man, I'm dying. (*Beat.*) Jimmy!

JIMMY: (*Offstage.*) Fuck off...ain't ad a piss fer hours.

TARIQ: Please man...

JIMMY comes out of a doorway. He is wiping his hands on his designer jeans, sunglasses resting on his head. Wears a dark blue bomber jacket and carries a mobile phone. TARIQ runs towards doorway, clutching his stomach.

Aaarruuh...

JIMMY: What's wrong with ya?

TARIQ: I'm constipated.

JIMMY: Constipated my black arse...not the turd that's blocked your colon mate.

TARIQ: Aaaruuh... Build us a spliff.

JIMMY: You can't eat and you can never shit.

TARIQ: Your Evy don't like us shitting in the shop bog... (*Moans.*)

JIMMY: She ain't mine. Works fer us that's all.

TARIQ: Says we do it like we're still sitting on bricks in the jungle... Aaruuh!

JIMMY: Funny...she don't mind givin' all the Pakis blow-jobs.

TARIQ comes out of closet clutching his stomach.

TARIQ: Like your dad?

JIMMY throws a bottle at TARIQ and he ducks.

JIMMY: She works for him...she's a qualified manager you sad...

TARIQ: Yeah…trained at 101 Taxis on Alum Rock Road.

JIMMY: What's needlin' ya Tariq… Like old women do ya… I could have a word.

TARIQ: Only if yer dad don't mind…

JIMMY: You little… I should…

TARIQ: What…should ya gimme a kiss? (*Puckers up.*)

JIMMY: That devil potion's bewitched ya…'s what it is…your head's cabbaged.

TARIQ: Ain't nothing wrong with it.

JIMMY: D'you wash your arse?

TARIQ: You what?

JIMMY: With the lautaa…'s what it's there for.

TARIQ: Shur'up man.

JIMMY: No…you couldn't have…you dirty…pig… Cleanliness is next to godliness…you never heard that before?

TARIQ: You a maulvi [priest/imam] now?

JIMMY: At least I'm not a smackhead man.

TARIQ: You smoke draw.

JIMMY: Don't say nothing in the Qur'an about hash!

TARIQ: It's nushaa…still gets you high.

JIMMY: I read Jum'aa every Friday…while you're burning the gear.

TARIQ: So you're a hypocrite?

JIMMY: Don't call me a hypocrite you non-believer kaafur.

TARIQ tosses the bag of powder to JIMMY as he pulls a spliff end from behind his ear.

TARIQ: Haven't we got work to do?

JIMMY: That's it…back out when you're losing an argument.

Beat. TARIQ lights his spliff and takes a drag.

TARIQ: Think you're such a good muslim.

JIMMY: Allah isn't against me workin' for a living.

TARIQ: Why don't you get a job in the bakery then?

JIMMY: Why don't you get off the gear?

Enter KERRY, JIMMY's girlfriend. She is wearing boots with a pointy, noisy heel. Her mousy hair is scraped into a very tight ponytail at the top of her head

KERRY: Alright Taz.

TARIQ: Alright Kez.

KERRY: Cup o' tea darlin?

JIMMY: Kettle's in the kitchen.

KERRY kisses him and sits down.

KERRY: Love you too. Plottin' were ya? The two of ya… buildin' up the family business?

TARIQ: Drugs and dollars that's it.

JIMMY: Shut it.

KERRY: How you're gonna import the gear from your end?

TARIQ: Our end?

JIMMY: Shut up Kerry.

KERRY: Pakistan…Jimmy's tekin' me with him when he goes.

TARIQ: It's not Pakistan. It's Azad Kashmir…that means 'free', d'you get it?

KERRY: Our John says it's the prettiest place in the world, all snowy mountains and 'ouses on the water, see I 'ave to go or 'e'll end up marryin' a beautiful virgin from the villages.

Then I'll ave no chance…you know cos your women they treat their 'usbands like gods don't they?

JIMMY: Can't you pack it in?

KERRY: I'm just tellin' Taz that we're gonna get married in Free Kashmir.

TARIQ: The country's called Kashmir.

KERRY: Make yer mind up… I'm gonna meet yer folks and get blessed by yer granny.

TARIQ: She'll bless you alright…with the end of her dundaa! [stick]

There is a knock on the door.

JIMMY: You expectin' anyone T?

KERRY: Quiet!

TARIQ falls off the sofa onto the floor, still smoking.

DEEMA: Jimmy, Tariq, it's me Deema, open the door.

JIMMY kicks TARIQ.

JIMMY: You prick, what's she doin' ere?

More banging. JIMMY gets up. He and KERRY start clearing things away.

DEEMA: Jimmy.

JIMMY: 'Ang on, I'm comin.

KERRY: C'mon Tariq…bloody lightweights.

TARIQ: I ain't feelin' well Kez.

KERRY: Get up you idiot.

KERRY picks TARIQ up and they exit. She shuts him into the toilet and JIMMY opens the front door as she exits into the kitchen. DEEMA walks in.

DEEMA: What took you so long? Couldn't hear me?

JIMMY: I was busy.

DEEMA: Half the block heard.

JIMMY: You should let a person know.

DEEMA: Where is he?

JIMMY: Who?

DEEMA: Your mate Tariq.

JIMMY: Ain't seen him.

DEEMA: Just tell me.

JIMMY: I was sleeping.

DEEMA: Tell me and I'll go.

JIMMY: I was in bed.

DEEMA: Just wanna talk to him.

KERRY enters, carrying a small plate of chocolate digestive biscuits

KERRY: Oh 'ello, this your bit on the side babe?

JIMMY: Shut it Kez, this is Tariq's sister Deema.

KERRY: Ah that's nice…I was just putting the tea on.

DEEMA: I was looking for my brother actually…didn't mean to disturb ya. Just that I can't find him anywhere.

KERRY: You're welcome to stop isn't she?

JIMMY: Er…

KERRY: Me and Jimmy were… Well you disturbed us…not in the mood any more do you know what I mean? (*Implying she and JIMMY had been in bed.*) Want a choccy biccy?

DEEMA: (*Unnerved.*) Pardon? Nothing…I don't want anything.

KERRY: Please yerself.

KERRY exits and DEEMA turns to leave with JIMMY following her.

JIMMY: You don't have to go… Stop here if you want.

DEEMA: You've got company. I didn't mean to barge in.

JIMMY: She'll be gone in a minute.

DEEMA: It ain't my business…just looking for my brother.

JIMMY: Check the flat if you don't believe me.

DEEMA: Forget it…look…if you see him…

JIMMY: I won't.

DEEMA: If you do… (*Beat.*) Tell him he needs to come home. It's important.

JIMMY: Anythin' I can help with?

DEEMA: No.

JIMMY: Wait a minute…

DEEMA: Just tell him will ya?

DEEMA goes to leave as JIMMY grabs his jacket.

JIMMY: Hang on. You don't wanna go out there. Can't trust people round here. You know me, always looked out for ya ain't I?

DEEMA: I looked out fer myself.

JIMMY: I'll look after you now.

DEEMA: I don't need looking after.

JIMMY: No…course you don't…

DEEMA: It's important right. You tell him.

JIMMY: You sure I can't help?

DEEMA: I just said. There's nothing you can do.

JIMMY: I'm offerin' that's all.

> *Beat.*

DEEMA: Course…it's family stuff.

JIMMY: And ain't I?

DEEMA: Yeah but…it's not that I don't appreciate your… It's just…we've got a bit of money trouble. / It ain't your job.

JIMMY: Why didn't you say? (*JIMMY grabs his jacket.*) Tell you what…let's take a drive down the high street.

DEEMA: You don't mind.

JIMMY: I'm headin' out anyway.

DEEMA: You sure?

JIMMY: Course. Probably in some caf…

DEEMA: You don't have to.

JIMMY: I want to.

> *They are leaving as KERRY enters with two mugs of tea.*

KERRY: You off then?

JIMMY: Just droppin' my cousin off Kez. Make sure that thing's done, okay?

> *JIMMY and DEEMA exit, and as they do, KERRY allows TARIQ out of the toilet. He stumbles out, retching from the smell.*

KERRY: What's wrong with 'er?

TARIQ: Fucken stinks in there.

KERRY: Pretty though…got lovely thick black hair and those big brown eyes, d'you think she's got the hots fer 'im? (*Ruffles his hair.*) D'you think Jimmy's got an admirer?

TARIQ: Pack it in Kes…let's sort the gear out.

KERRY: Right y'are Godfather…

KERRY starts laughing.

Lights down.

SCENE FOUR

Living room of the Chaudhry home. Morning, a week later. RAFIQUE is sitting on a chair, reading a newspaper. He is wearing a light-coloured shalwar kameez; ZAINAB, a pale green suit with baggy white cardigan.

ZAINAB enters with a tray and a colander carrying a small cucumber, potatoes, a peeler and a knife. She almost trips over a box in her way.

RAFIQUE: Look where you're going.

ZAINAB looks at RAFIQUE and puts the tray down.

ZAINAB: I can't keep them here.

RAFIQUE: So much space in this house and you're moaning about a few boxes.

ZAINAB picks up the knife. Beat. ZAINAB picks up the cucumber, slices it and passes a piece to RAFIQUE.

ZAINAB: Taste them…from the garden. It is sweeter than the shop ones.

RAFIQUE: Vegetables should be grown in fields, rows of them, a view of abundance outside your window. This country, for ten months of the year, it's a bastard place but when the sun comes out, it's like holy water to the sick and dying.

ZAINAB: You went to the farm.

RAFIQUE: We will have miles of carrots, potatoes, tomatoes and when you pick them they should be fatter than both your hands.

ZAINAB: This will not grow on your English farm. (*She presents a pot containing a small, leafy plant.*) You don't recognise the leaves?

RAFIQUE: Raath Kee Rani.

RAFIQUE recites the fourth line of Nasir Kaazmi's ghazal beginning 'Zabaan sakhun ko, sakhun baankpan ko tarsega…'. ZAINAB joins him and together they recite the fifth line.

ZAINAB takes the pot from RAFIQUE and sets it next to her as she begins to peel the potatoes.

Such a 'shareef' sensible child isn't it…Mahmood's boy?

ZAINAB: Jamil? You know what people say?

RAFIQUE: What do they say? People are jealous of success…it is Mahmood's kismet to have a clever boy and everybody must tell lies about him.

ZAINAB: It wasn't me.

RAFIQUE: He would be a fine partner for any young woman.

ZAINAB: I am sure.

RAFIQUE: What do you think?

ZAINAB: About?

RAFIQUE: We have to do our duty…and how many problems would go…

ZAINAB: My Deema?

RAFIQUE: Mine too…she would be happy I believe… The boy likes her…

ZAINAB: You should talk to her.

RAFIQUE: You are the mother… No matter…who are we to say, when the time is right, it will be right.

ZAINAB stops peeling, takes the colander and goes to throw the peelings in a nearby plastic bag, near a box. She picks up a book.

ZAINAB: Cooking?

RAFIQUE: You didn't see? Recipe book, 'Easy Meals in a Hurry'.

ZAINAB: Nice photos.

RAFIQUE: Best quality paper, two hundred recipes, breakfast, lunch and dinner.

ZAINAB: Is that bacon?

ZAINAB flashes a picture of a traditional English fry-up.

RAFIQUE: Ghaureh [white people] have to eat as well.

ZAINAB: There must be.

RAFIQUE: Five hundred.

DEEMA: Five hundred books?

ZAINAB: Where will the visitors sit?

RAFIQUE: They will be gone in a few days. Wonderful eh? Bargain I tell you…five pound each one.

ZAINAB: Paanj pound? What did you pay him with?

RAFIQUE: I'll sell them for ten pounds, that's a fair price.

ZAINAB: Who will buy bacon photos in this area?

RAFIQUE: Don't be so narrow-minded. These are modern times Zainab. There are recipes for sandwiches, salads, soups. All the forward-thinking young girls will want them. In a few months our troubles will be over… I have calculated it…five hundred times ten equals five thousand. I give half to Mahmood and half I keep…then I will order more from Khan Sahib and only then.

ZAINAB: These are English books. Nobody on this street speaks English.

RAFIQUE: You have learnt nothing from living in this country for thirty-five years.

ZAINAB: Who is going to pay your stupid money and who will give their husband egg and bacon sandwich?

RAFIQUE: Instead of bacon use potato. Karim's wife is very fast. She will like and Maulvi Amjad's daughter…did you know she's training to be a chef?

ZAINAB: We have to do something.

RAFIQUE: Don't you worry. I have arranged it. Jamil is coming.

ZAINAB: He is going to pay Mr Dickson?

RAFIQUE: He is coming to see Deema.

ZAINAB: So the money is paid for the house?

RAFIQUE: One step at a time Zainab… I am working on it.

ZAINAB: I saw Abdul at Nadia's house last night. He tells me, in front of all the funeral guests: 'Zainab jee…your phone is out of order again…you have bad luck naa? My phone is tip-top.' I was ashamed I tell you. It is a struggle.

RAFIQUE: Struggle is part of life Zainab. My blood runs through me as hot and dark and fast as if I were thirty. Sometimes I put my hand to my chest and feel my heart jumping, dancing… Push on old man. You are not beaten yet. You are not on your knees yet. You are free. This heart is an expert at taking blows. You think a few thousand pounds will stop me in my tracks? You think Mr Dickson will beat me? When I am sitting on my land…

ZAINAB: I have waited many years for that…

RAFIQUE: Zainab jee. We must have hope. We must keep trying.

ZAINAB: And stupid fools who failed school are the paisaa-wallahs [ones with money] while you Professor Sahib… The uncles and cousins who worked in the bakeries and the mills have kitchen extensions and mansions in Mirpur…the factory-workers are nawabs…

37

RAFIQUE: Factory? I am a teacher, did you forget?

ZAINAB: Did you ever teach anyone? I forget.

RAFIQUE: You don't just take the scraps they throw at you. Respect must come first.

ZAINAB: Other mothers have married eight, naa, ten children on their husband's factory wages.

RAFIQUE: They don't see how it degrades a man. You are my wife. We have a home. My children must look to me as an example.

ZAINAB: Our friends and our parents have been kind.

RAFIQUE: What about the bookstore in Balsall Heath? How many days I sat and waited for customers?

ZAINAB: While you sit and wait what do we eat?

RAFIQUE: In all these years I never worked? I didn't apply for jobs?

ZAINAB: Two if I remember…three weeks at the Urdu college and many years translating essays for nothing but praise… Oh clever Rafique Sahib they all say.

RAFIQUE: Because I have ambition I must suffer?

ZAINAB: Ten summers ago, when Khan Doctor told you he will build a school if you will be head teacher. You never did. He begged me, 'Make him change his mind. Think Zainab jee, your fortunes will be transformed.' 'Who am I?' I told him.

RAFIQUE: That was not a small responsibility…a thing so…so big. If it all goes wrong you will say it is my fault.

ZAINAB: I am not scared to work if you let me.

RAFIQUE: Again the same thing…they would finish you off out there and what would you get? Two pounds an hour, sweeping floors?

ZAINAB: One day's work at a time Deema's ubaa. That is how money is made.

RAFIQUE: You will see…a few years from now, no, mark this day you hear…two years from this day, I will call Mahmood, Arifa, that bastard Abdul…our brothers and sisters and Dickson Sahib…I will invite them and throw the biggest party on our fifty acres. I will watch as they eat the finest khanna [food] I have provided…ten, no, twenty different dishes… Then I shall take them on a tour of the stables where they will praise the horses with jealous eyes and the orchards where they can pick their choice of fruit. After we will serve Kashmiri tea, the colour of roses and the finest cream cakes and when they sit in disbelief and stare like owls, I will smile. It will be a smile that is set like paper on glue. It will stretch from this ear to this ear. You will believe me then? You will say, why did I, how could I doubt this man? Did I not know what he was capable of? And they will say, 'Would you know it…Rafique has outdone us…how small our vision…how near our aims.'

ZAINAB has finished chopping the potatoes. She holds the knife steady as DEEMA enters the room, carrying her envelope and speaking on her mobile phone.

ZAINAB: Shall I bring the saag?

DEEMA: (*On phone.*) Sorry about that.

RAFIQUE: No…no, why wait any longer? I'm going to Barber Majid. He has many customers. So what if I make nine pounds. The first step is the hardest they say.

RAFIQUE exits and DEEMA is still on the phone.

DEEMA: This is the best way to get hold of me. The builders cut the phone cables… Yes, I know…but thank you, bye.

ZAINAB has stood up and is looking at a box with the knife in her hands.

They said my application was impeccable.

ZAINAB: Come on, help me.

DEEMA: Did you hear me? I'm down to the last hundred.

ZAINAB: Is good. Come. We have to move them to the back-room cupboard.

DEEMA puts her phone and envelope down.

DEEMA: There's nowhere to put them.

ZAINAB: He is going to sell them.

DEEMA: To who? They're crap.

ZAINAB: (*Still pushing.*) Allah is going to help him.

DEEMA: You can't lift that.

ZAINAB: I want them away.

DEEMA holds ZAINAB's arms.

DEEMA: I'll get Tariq to do it with me.

ZAINAB: He can't lift himself…

DEEMA: Wait…at least until I get back okay?

ZAINAB: (*Struggling and breathless.*) You take the other side.

DEEMA: Umee, wait…

ZAINAB pushes DEEMA away and stabs at the box with the knife she is carrying. She throws it down and DEEMA picks it up.

ZAINAB: They are in my way. Boxes and books and papers and bags all over. My garden is not a dump. This house is not a dump. I want all out of here…you understand? Out, out!

ZAINAB kicks the box and then hits herself on the head. DEEMA tries to grab her. She pulls at her dupatta and continues to slap herself and pull at her hair.

Get them out of here, please Deema please…all away from here. I want them gone. They're useless…useless!

ZAINAB flops onto a seat. Beat. DEEMA puts her bag down, takes her jacket off, sits down and faces her mum. Beat.

Lights down.

SCENE FIVE

KERRY's flat. Later that same afternoon. An electric-bar heater is on in the corner. It is screwed onto the wall. TARIQ is tottering about the room in his T-shirt and jogging bottoms, collecting his belongings: a jumper which he painstakingly brushes down and picks at to neaten, a martial arts magazine, a carrier bag in which he throws cigarette boxes (ten-packs), some containing pieces of blackened foil, loose lighters, tissue paper, some folded clean foil, Rizla paper and a bit of cannabis. Aziz Mian plays in the background.

TARIQ is loosening his baggy jumper as if it is clinging to him. He finally takes it off, folds it, sets it aside and lies down on the sofa. KERRY enters with a bottle of vodka and a carton of orange juice. There are a couple of glasses on the table.

TARIQ: It's boilin' in 'ere.

KERRY: Don't touch the heater.

TARIQ: I'm burnin' up.

KERRY: You were freezin' a minute ago.

TARIQ goes to turn the music off.

'Ang on, leave that.

TARIQ sits down again.

I wanna hear, it…calms me down. It's like they're singing their hearts out.

TARIQ: Cos they are… It's real mystical…like the Sufis…the qawwali, it's a song to God, thankin' 'im for everything we've got.

KERRY: Sometimes I wish I'd been born Pakistan, Taz.

TARIQ: Ain't about where you're born, it's where your heart is.

KERRY: Yeah, 's what I'm saying. I'd rather be Pakistan than Irish sometimes.

TARIQ: Pakistani… Pakistan's a country you div, anyway us lot ain't Pakistani, we're Kashmiri. There's a big difference you know.

KERRY: I'm always gonna love Our Lady, Mary, Mother of Jesus, but if I was gonna be another religion, I'd be Pakistan, I mean, Islam…muslim, like you lot.

TARIQ: We're all the same Kez, same God, all religion's fucked up and all religion's good ain't it?

KERRY: Your women and yer families, they all get looked after so well.

TARIQ: You've got yer freedom.

KERRY: (*Laughing.*) I ain't free. I'm a slave to the drink and the gear.

TARIQ: You know what I mean, you do as you please, goin' out, gettin' pissed up with yer friends, invitin' yer mates round for dinner, fucken parents buyin' you birthday presents.

KERRY: The only present I got was a box in the eye and a poundin' if I mentioned a bloke to Pete an' them.

TARIQ: That's cos you're a girl, same fer girls wherever you are.

TARIQ puts his jumper back on. Beat.

KERRY: Lads are twats aren't they? To think a couple o' pints in The Sailor gets 'em a shag down the back o' The Morris. Do you know what Tariq? How do they do it? Those pigs in their suits and their gold bracelets driving around with their wives in their big Mercs? I mean how do them women sleep with 'em after knowing – and they must know – the only time they shag their 'usbands is when 'e wants a kid… They must know what pigs they're sleeping with.

TARIQ: What are you on about?

KERRY: Our Lisa works the Rock.

TARIQ: She's a ho…a pros Kez, what's wrong with ya?

KERRY: She says the Pakis are the worst. She says they're always sniffing around tryin' to get freebies and the rich ones are the stingiest but they all like to get rough. Says you have to watch out for the fuckers. They like turn up, sardine-packed in the car and call 'em honkie bitches if they won't gang bang.

TARIQ: What you doin' with a Paki?

KERRY: He's different.

TARIQ: Different? That's new. So where is he then? Gone to see your Lisa has he?

KERRY: Business meeting actually.

TARIQ: You get off on it.

KERRY: Shut yer face you perv.

TARIQ: Jimmy the gangster…Jimmy who carts you around in his beamer and his jeep… It's a thing isn't it…the little scum all bow down to Jimmy so they all bow down to Jimmy's girl too… They can't mess with Jimmy's ho… that's just fer him…

KERRY holds a bottle as if she is about to whack TARIQ.

KERRY: I said take it back.

TARIQ: Fuck off you silly cow.

TARIQ gets up to put his coat on.

KERRY: Tariq.

TARIQ: I ain't your lackey Kerry. I'm not saying what you want to hear.

KERRY punches him on the head.

Oi you silly bitch.

They struggle and the bottle is flung onto the floor and they both end up there with KERRY lying on TARIQ.

KERRY: He's not like that.

TARIQ: He's a saint ain't he? What am I talkin' about? I forgot about the halo over his head…just miss it sometimes you know.

KERRY: He wouldn't attack a woman. He don't call women those words neither.

TARIQ pushes her off and gets up.

TARIQ: Good luck to ya.

TARIQ puts a hat on and a hood over his head.

KERRY: What d'you care anyway?

Beat.

TARIQ: Your 'ead needs fixin'.

KERRY: Runnin' off now…? Where you goin'?

TARIQ: To the offy for a Whole Nut but I don't need to do I? Got me one right fucken 'ere.

KERRY: Don't get all moody.

TARIQ: You are loose up there…no screws man…need lockin' up.

Beat.

KERRY: Din't mean to hurt ya.

TARIQ: You can see a psychiatrist on the NHS these days love.

KERRY: It's you who's a nutter… You jealous of Jimmy or somethin'?

TARIQ: Me? Jealous of a bloke everyone hates?

KERRY: That wanker at the offy. He says I was an alcoholic Taz… 'E ain't met you as 'e Taz? (*Beat.*) I'm not a big drinker. I don't 'ave to drink. Just a tot now an' again… I mean I've got the gear ain't I?

TARIQ: You shou'n't smoke. Jimmy'll kill me.

KERRY: He knows… Anyway Jimmy coun't kill a fly, got no balls. (*Beat.*) I reckon you have. A man should be a man, not a woman. It's about feelings ain't it? Jimmy wou'n't listen to songs like that. A warm heart. In a warm bed. You got a warm bed 'ave ya?

TARIQ: Like you're interested. You're Jimmy's girl anyway.

KERRY: Course not… Bet you ain't even got a bed 'ave ya?

TARIQ takes the spliff and bends down holding it in front of KERRY.

TARIQ: That's for you to find out.

KERRY: Cheeky.

Momentarily they stare at each other, then TARIQ rises again.

TARIQ: We've gotta make sure he don't find out we had some.

KERRY: Get me a lager.

TARIQ: Only got a quid.

KERRY: I got some of my giro, get a big bottle. He is still the cheapest round 'ere even if he looks down his nose.

TARIQ: You mad? I ain't payin' him.

KERRY: He'll watch ya like you've walked in with a bomb.

TARIQ: Fuck him. Fuck arseholes lookin' down their noses at ya just cos they've been donkeys all their lives. Workin' in shit for shit. You know what I'd like Kerry…work abroad, you can make money abroad you know. 'Ave a few quid, go an' see a film, lie in the sun, maybe get married, settle down with a good woman who talks to ya…get her a nice pair of Carvela shoes, like those toffee-nosed fuckers in Rackhams, a couple o' kids, give 'em Timberland clothes… maybe have a little car you know? What sort of God is there, lets bastards like that 'ave money and leaves good people with nothing?

KERRY: The only way you'll 'ave money is if you rob a bank or summink

TARIQ: I can do it easy.

KERRY: People like you an' me…there's no room fer us.

TARIQ: Jimmy's got money.

KERRY: Jimmy's a bastard and I'm a bitch. That's why we'll get by.

TARIQ: I ain't lettin' people walk over me all my life. It's not gonna happen to me.

KERRY: Maybe if you pray hard enough. Our mom, she always said her 'Hail Marys' first thing in the morning an' last thing at night. Wou'n't go to church though. Said there were more sinners inside a house of God than in the streets outside. But you lot don't go to church.

TARIQ: Yeah we do. Mosques are just like churches…only warmer and brighter. But we don't 'ave to go. We can pray wherever we are. I'm praying now.

TARIQ is staring blankly at the wall. Beat.

KERRY: 'Ave you ever had the Lord Jesus Christ come to you? (*Beat.*) 'E came to me…just after our mom passed away. I was sitting by 'er. She was lyin' flat out in our sittin' room in a cheap cardboard coffin. Pete had nicked the money for the funeral. Our dad was runnin' round the 'ouse with little Michael's cricket bat, 'Where is he that son of a whore!'

he was screamin', chasin' Pete up an' down the stairs, an' out the back o' the 'ouse... Din't see him fer a year. We got slapped if we ever mentioned his name.

TARIQ: How could 'e?

KERRY: He'd drank the money for the coffin and the gravestone.

TARIQ: 'Is own mother. One thing if she's alive but 'is dead mother.

KERRY: Oh shut up Taz...'e was all cut up cos she was dead.

TARIQ: You're mad.

KERRY: No. I forgave him...Jesus told me to. (*Beat.*) An' then 'e told me to leave and never come back to that 'ouse. Said I couldn't wash away sins I didn't commit. (*Beat.*) S'pose if 'e was your religion, then 'e wou'n't 'ave done it...you know, not bein' allowed to drink an' all. He wouldn'a got tempted.

TARIQ: Would you say you knew a lot of our religion?

KERRY: A few.

TARIQ: So how many of 'em you know don't drink?

KERRY: Dunno.

TARIQ: That's cos the ones you know all do so that's your theory in shit.

KERRY: No it ain't.

TARIQ: All sell their moms out at the first chance.

KERRY: That's just you scummy druggy lot.

TARIQ: So why are you with Jimmy, I mean what does he give you?

KERRY: He looks after me, he loves me, he's gonna...he's gonna marry me.

TARIQ: Your Jimmy is marrying his inbred first cousin from back home, just like Jimmy's old man and 'er old man an' my old man did.

KERRY: You're a sad case.

TARIQ: Ask him…d'you wan' any chocolate for the last time?

KERRY gets up and starts pulling on a coat.

KERRY: Don't want any of your bastard chocolate…I'll get my own.

TARIQ: Fine with me.

KERRY: You know you people. You're against nature. It's not right. No wonder so many of ya carry on like fucken spastics.

TARIQ: That is out of order.

KERRY: Just cos he's got his life together…he's gonna marry me in Free Kashmir and he's gonna buy me a shop.

TARIQ: You'll be his skivvy, sellin' corned beef to old men who stink o' piss.

KERRY: Sad old Taz, Jimmy's little runner.

TARIQ: That's gonna change.

KERRY: Old habits.

TARIQ: That's what you think.

KERRY: Treats ya like shit, always pays ya short and you just carry on pickin' up, droppin' off and doin' any dirty little jobs he throws at ya… Let him walk all over ya.

TARIQ: I know what I'm doin' alright?

KERRY: You should wake up. No one's that loyal.

TARIQ: As if you give a…

KERRY: I don't.

TARIQ: I ain't no softie right.

KERRY: You ain't bad. I know you ain't. Got nice eyes.

TARIQ: Oh yeah? Better than Jimmy's?

Beat.

KERRY: They're kind… Bet they were proper bright and shiny once.

TARIQ: Eh? They still are…see?

KERRY: Yeah…kind of.

Beat.

TARIQ: What about 'is money? You ever been tempted?

KERRY: I get what I want.

TARIQ: Better to have yer own than to wait on hand-outs.

KERRY: Beggars wait on hand-outs. I ain't no beggar. Jimmy's money is my money alright?

TARIQ: Do you know where he keeps it?

KERRY: (*Laughs.*) Think I'm a plank?

TARIQ: You said he tells you everything.

KERRY: So I'm gonna tell the first div that asks.

TARIQ: You think he'd trust his future wife.

KERRY: He does.

TARIQ: Don't look like it.

KERRY: It ain't workin' Taz.

TARIQ: You must've watched him.

KERRY: I 'aven't.

TARIQ: Not once?

KERRY: Yer pissing me off now.

TARIQ: Just show us.

KERRY: I can't fucken show ya.

TARIQ: Thought not.

KERRY: I wou'n't if I could.

TARIQ: So you do know

KERRY: Fuck right off will ya.

TARIQ: You comin'?

KERRY: No.

TARIQ: C'mon…nick ya a bounty.

KERRY: Get lost.

TARIQ: An' a Twix then.

> *KERRY flings a crunched up can at him.*

I was only messin' about Kez. Come on, I'll get bored on
my own.

KERRY: One condition.

TARIQ: Go on then.

KERRY: Sing me that song…you know…the one we used to
hear when we were at school.

TARIQ: Fuck off!

KERRY: Come on Taz, or I'll stay here and tell Jimmy you 'ad
all his gear.

TARIQ: Don't be a bitch.

KERRY: I could call 'im…

TARIQ: I'll swap you…you tell me and I'll sing…

KERRY: Don't make no difference…you can't get it.

KERRY points to the electric-bar heater screwed to the wall.

TARIQ: In there? You serious? Stupid wanker…

KERRY: Not that stupid…no one's had it so far…

TARIQ: That's cos it's in your place… Maybe he ain't so stupid. Reckon he'd miss it?

KERRY: Unscrews the bloody thing every night and empties it every few days, the tosser. He'd miss it.

TARIQ: Got a screwdriver?

KERRY: Get lost.

TARIQ: I'm joking.

KERRY: The song Tariq.

TARIQ: Alright, alright. 'Aap Jaisa koi mairee zindagi naa ayee, Baath bun jaye…'

KERRY: Uhuh uhuh.

TARIQ: 'Baath bun jayee…'

KERRY: 'Bot ban jai! Bot ban jai!' Once more go on…

TARIQ: No man…

KERRY: I'll sing it with ya…go on.

KERRY puts her arms round TARIQ as he sings the verse again, stopping to look back at the place where the money is. They both sound terrible, and as they exit the sound of 'Aap Jaisa Koi' by Nazia Hussan fades out.

SCENE SIX

Two days later. The garden of the Chaudhry home. It is about four in the afternoon. The boxes are stacked up on one side of the garden in as neat a section as possible.

DEEMA walks in with a French language book. She is walking and reading a page. RAFIQUE is holding a hand-held mirror and plucking stray nose hairs. His legs are outstretched. However, he is wearing a cotton shalwar kameez. ZAINAB is sweeping the area with a broom.

DEEMA: Dad.

RAFIQUE pulls out a hair. It is painful.

RAFIQUE: Ow…eh?

DEEMA: Move your feet a sec.

RAFIQUE shifts to one side as DEEMA is free to walk past him. ZAINAB sweeps up the dust and puts it into a bag which she puts down in a corner.

RAFIQUE: Nothing from the bank Zainab?

ZAINAB: Only this for Deema.

DEEMA sits down and starts to look through the contents of the envelope.

RAFIQUE: I should have heard by now… Six books he wants.

ZAINAB: The bank manager?

RAFIQUE: And so? I showed and he liked.

DEEMA: You serious?

RAFIQUE: For him I will do special cheap rate but think of all his rich friends…

ZAINAB: And the mortgage.

RAFIQUE: He is a reasonable person… He will do his best.

ZAINAB: Deema's ubaa…he doesn't own the bank.

RAFIQUE: Leave it Zainab. You don't know about these matters. You think they are not at it all the time? This nation invented corruption. It is their countries that have taught our nations. You think I don't know?

ZAINAB: A few books won't change anything.

RAFIQUE: Don't underestimate me. That has always been their mistake. I have learnt a thing or two in my time. I will show them.

ZAINAB: Choop…that is why your daughter is doing now… listening to your big talk… Ask her what she has done.

DEEMA: I haven't done anything.

ZAINAB: Tell him.

RAFIQUE: Deema?

DEEMA: The careers fair…I did some tests…got through to the first stage…

RAFIQUE: And so? That is admirable nah?

DEEMA: They said they wanna see me… I've got an interview.

RAFIQUE: Subhanallah. [Thanks be to God.] Fantastic.

ZAINAB: Who said?

DEEMA: The airline… Cabin crew.

RAFIQUE: Cabin crew. (*Clears his throat.*) You must think carefully. We will talk later. I have to get ready.

RAFIQUE exits.

ZAINAB: Kooriyeh [girl]…clear the dishes.

DEEMA doesn't move.

DEEMA: It's well paid and I get loads of time off. (*Beat.*) Why can't you be pleased for me?

ZAINAB: And what do I explain the friends, the neighbours, your family…why my children run from me.

DEEMA: I'm not.

ZAINAB: People will say, fikur naa karr. [don't you worry]

DEEMA: People can say what they like…

ZAINAB: You want to cut off from the world.

DEEMA: I want to see the world umee.

ZAINAB: You are big enough now. Use your head. A job is good but a job is not enough. We are made to share our lives.

DEEMA: I'm not getting married.

ZAINAB: So big and so stupid… A woman cannot live in this world without a man.

DEEMA: Don't you ever wish you did?

ZAINAB starts to gather the dishes.

Don't you mom? Are you happy? What if all those years ago when you married dad?

ZAINAB: What do you know of that? Do you think they asked me if I liked him? Do you think they showed me a photo and I was happy to marry handsome Rafique Sahib? We did what we were to do. We would never hurt our parents.

We hear the door open and muffled sounds offstage. RAFIQUE enters with JIMMY in tow. RAFIQUE has changed into a badly fitting shirt and polyester suit. He has smartened his hair.

RAFIQUE: You are getting ready Zainab?

ZAINAB: Oh…sorry.

JIMMY: Salaam aunty.

ZAINAB: Oh poothar… I just change.

RAFIQUE: You two young people. Why don't you talk about your plans?

DEEMA: Dad?

ZAINAB: Might be Jamil has tea Deema?

JIMMY: No thanks. Can't stop long.

DEEMA: Mom?

ZAINAB exits with RAFIQUE.

What plans?

JIMMY: So where's Tariq?

DEEMA: I dunno.

JIMMY: He home?

DEEMA: I ain't seen him…

JIMMY: Best have a look myself then.

DEEMA: He's not here.

JIMMY: Thought you said you hadn't seen him.

DEEMA: He hasn't been here for weeks. Thought he was with you.

JIMMY: I've been looking for him fer three days.

DEEMA: What is it you want?

JIMMY: Cup of chaa would be nice.

DEEMA: My mum asked.

JIMMY: Din't want it then.

JIMMY lights a cigarette and offers DEEMA one.

DEEMA: No thank you.

JIMMY: I like politeness. People don't rate it enough. Reckon it tells you a lot about a person… Got an ashtray?

JIMMY flicks ash onto the ground.

Thing is the tea I like takes time. No kuchee [weak] dip the teabag in and pull it out. D'you know what I mean? Sweet milky brown pukkee chaa…slowly boiled, plenty of masala.

Gotta take your dad to meet my dad see? So he can beg some more money off him.

DEEMA: What is you fuckin' problem?

JIMMY: You Chaudhry's think you're above everyone. Think with your clever banter and smilin' faces you can con people…

DEEMA: My dad's never conned anyone.

JIMMY: Nah, he just begs. Now can you tell me where he's hidin'?

DEEMA: Need him to get rid of more drugs?

JIMMY: Oh, he's done too much of that already…he's been very silly.

DEEMA: And you had nothing to do with it?

JIMMY: Your brother's a junkie all on his own Deema. Nobody made him one. The idiot can't even keep to the first rule.

DEEMA: Course. You just peddle it to pay for your fake designer gear. Does it feel good to drive down the Rock in your flash car?

JIMMY: I should shove your head in that tandoor right now.

DEEMA: I should kick yours out.

JIMMY: Okay…I got carried away… Don't mean that stuff… It's just…this isn't your problem…but… The thing is Tariq has nicked my money and I've got people who need paying.

DEEMA: I don't know what the two of you get up to but…

JIMMY: Nine grand actually. You tell him he better come find me. (*Beat.*) Cos I will find him you get me sis?

JIMMY looks DEEMA up and down.

You're not bad looking for a Paki bird, d'you know that?

ZAINAB enters dressed in a new salwar kameez outfit: pale blue and new cardigan.

ZAINAB: Sorry poothar…I come and see your mother.

JIMMY: Jee? That's cool auntyjee.

ZAINAB: Deema…we come home late. Make sure doors are locked.

They exit and DEEMA goes to the chair and sits down. She takes a letter from the envelope. She stares at the page. She rips it in half, then rips it again and scrunches it into a ball. She throws it towards the rubbish ZAINAB cleared earlier. She sits forward, wrapping her arms around herself.

Lights down.

SCENE SEVEN

City street, early evening, a few days later. DEEMA is walking behind TARIQ, a slight figure in too many clothes, wearing a battered hooded raincoat which is too big for him.

DEEMA: Oi.

TARIQ jumps.

TARIQ: For fuck's sake…what are you doin' here?

DEEMA: I was passin'.

TARIQ: You flippin' followin' me?

DEEMA: Said I was passin' and I needed to talk to you.

TARIQ: You're going on like some sort of nutter Deem. I'm alright.

DEEMA: No you're not.

TARIQ: We'll talk about it later right.

TARIQ stops to lean against a wall.

DEEMA: We can't talk about it later.

TARIQ: Please man…my legs are killin' me.

DEEMA: Mom and dad…we've got some trouble at home.

TARIQ: Aaah! Fuck.

DEEMA: What is wrong with you?

TARIQ: Legs are hurting…like someone's driven over 'em with a truck.

DEEMA leans next to him and starts to roll a cigarette.

Can I have one?

DEEMA passes him the rolled-up cigarette. TARIQ takes a drag and bends over then tries to stretch, all the time acting as if he's dying. DEEMA is motionless.

DEEMA: It's your own doing.

TARIQ: Need your help…I'm desperate.

DEEMA: You're always desperate. Meanwhile I go to college, apply for jobs, get the shopping mum needs, help pay the bills, wash the dishes, make the roti…tell dad lies about where you are…

TARIQ: Didn't ask you to. Did I ask you?

DEEMA: There's enough to think about.

TARIQ: It ain't that bad.

DEEMA: Yes it is.

TARIQ: Stop makin' a big deal or everything man. In time…

DEEMA: We've got no time. The house is being repossessed..

TARIQ: Just scare tactics.

DEEMA: How is dad gonna get the money?

TARIQ: Bastard…

Deema: What…?

TARIQ is hitting his head with his hands.

TARIQ: I can't walk…feels like I'm dying…if I don't…if I don't get it…I…I'm gonna end up doin' something stupid…can't even sit down. Some dog tried to bite my arse.

DEEMA: See I don't think I can take any more of all this shit… I just can't deal with it.

TARIQ: You should've seen it. Fucken great mangy thing… down by the railway bridge… Was just walkin' past this 'ouse…I mean the front door…it was open and nobody was around… People round 'ere take silly chances man… I walk up to it…tryin' to be a good neighbour…and this woman sets her Alsatian on me. He's going for me like he ain't eaten for days and she's flapping her arms up and down screamin' thieves like me should go back to their own country… I'm goin': I was born 'ere bitch… The cheek of it Deem…she's the one who should have been locked up… I mean I could get rabies…I should get rabies…then I'd sue her arse.

DEEMA: Shut up Tariq…I've had it with ya…try my hardest and I mess it up. All this trouble. I had an interview… cabin crew…I could've bin seeing Rome, Paris…bloody Marrakech.

TARIQ: What interview?

DEEMA: It don't matter.

DEEMA sits on the ground and TARIQ calms down, slowly making his way down to her clutching his leg as he does.

TARIQ: C'mon sis…that's wicked. You know dad…last minute something'll turn up. You'll see…and you've got a job… that's good…you've gotta think about yerself. That's what I'm gonna do.

DEEMA: I haven't got a job.

TARIQ: You just said man.

DEEMA: I had an interview Tariq.

TARIQ: You'll get it no probs.

DEEMA: I cancelled okay. Said I couldn't go.

Beat.

TARIQ: What you do that for?

DEEMA: Jimmy came round for ya.

TARIQ: Fuck him.

DEEMA: He threatened me Tariq…

TARIQ: What's the arsehole said…I'll –

DEEMA: Said he wants the money you took.

TARIQ: What you talking about?

DEEMA: I'm speaking a foreign language ain't I? You can't get out of this one. He's angry. Said he's gonna sort you out. In mum's house Tariq… You're gonna drag them into it…what the fuck are you doing?

TARIQ: I'm fixing things Deem.

DEEMA: He isn't gonna go away. Dunno what he could do.

TARIQ: All mouth man. Jimmy ain't even bin inside. He's a wannabe.

DEEMA: They don't need this… We've got other shit to do. I've got other shit to do Tariq… Just get him his money… You have still got it ain't ya?

TARIQ: I haven't got his fuckin' money man.

DEEMA: How long you gonna hide for?

TARIQ: Listen to me. I'm gonna give this up…I'm gonna detox. I've gotta be there with ya…start working… Fed up with all this…you don't know how fed up I am. I went to the clinic.

DEEMA: You did.

TARIQ: Told ya…I ain't messin' about.

DEEMA: Just come see mum and dad right. Maybe we can deal with it together.

TARIQ: It's all gonna change. Don't want to be like this any more.

DEEMA: That's good Taz.

TARIQ: I've bee cutting down… By next week, I'll be almost clean…but it's fuckin' hurtin' sis. I need a bit of money… just to get enough to cover the pain

DEEMA stands up chucking her cigarette away.

DEEMA: Have to go.

TARIQ: So can you help us?

DEEMA: With what Tariq?

TARIQ: You heard what I said man…

DEEMA: Ain't got nothing.

TARIQ: Your wages.

DEEMA: My wages.

TARIQ: Twenny quid that's all.

DEEMA: We have to get the phone reconnected.

TARIQ pulls out his giro book, stuffed in the back of his jeans pocket and hands it to her. Beat.

TARIQ: It's due a week today. / You collect it and take your cut.

DEEMA: Next week.

TARIQ: Please. (*Beat.*) You watch…it's all gonna change. Stop worrying and do your work. You can't keep takin' everythin' to heart. We know what we're doing.

DEEMA: You'll come home? See if we can sort this out?

TARIQ: Told you…I'll see mum, talk to dad…say hello an' that.

Beat.

DEEMA: Yeah?

TARIQ: Yeah.

DEEMA takes his hand and he pulls away.

TARIQ: I'm not a kid man. (*Beat.*) Can I still 'ave that score then?

Lights fade.

SCENE EIGHT

Chaudhry home indoors. Midday the next day. RAFIQUE and DEEMA are eating lunch. A couple of boxes are in the room. On the table are fresh chappatis, wrapped in a tea-towel in a changair [flat, straw plate], a jug of water, glasses, sliced apples and oranges on a plate. A small bowl of chicken curry.

TARIQ has a chappati in his hand and picks at the curry every now and then. He is walking about as if restless.

TARIQ: So what's with the boxes?

Beat.

They off the back of a lorry?

RAFIQUE: That is my stock.

TARIQ: Stock?

DEEMA: He's gonna sell them.

ZAINAB enters with a roll of kitchen towels and sets them down. They all move along to make room for ZAINAB to sit down.

Come and sit umee.

ZAINAB squashes in alongside RAFIQUE. She offers RAFIQUE the plate of cut fruit. He lingers before taking a slice of apple.

ZAINAB: (*To TARIQ.*) Come moondiyaah. [boy]

TARIQ stops wandering and sits down. He dips his chappati in his curry and eats.

I will build a small greenhouse by the choley. [chick peas]

RAFIQUE: Saaed's boy has a greenhouse...many of them. Who could think...he could never get his puttee [alphabet] right at school and now he is father to a computer millionaire rich kid.

DEEMA: Whizz-kid.

RAFIQUE: Same thing...they are clever and fast with money, isn't it?

DEEMA: Has Mr Dickson been round again?

ZAINAB: Court date in the post.

RAFIQUE: I will sort it out.

ZAINAB: Sell them... Give him some pennies.

RAFIQUE: You people do not know. It takes time to build a new business. Jamil will pick them up. I will speak to him.

ZAINAB: Jimmy is going to give you three thousand pounds heh?

RAFIQUE: He is a whizz-kid. He knows he will double his return.

ZAINAB: His mother was shopping in Apnaa stores on Saturday...bags of silk for new season suits. What does she have to worry about? Her son puts money in her hands. She says to me, 'I have to fight him painjee, I do not need money. I have everything but my Jamil, he will not smile unless I buy a new suit every month and wear it.' Such a son cannot be a crook or a beggar.

TARIQ: So which one am I?

ZAINAB: Heh?

TARIQ: Crook or beggar?

RAFIQUE: Saaed's boy is going to buy the farm, get some chickens and go halal wholesale. He is a blessed man. It is all in your kismet and that lies with the great one above.

TARIQ: Maybe one day I'll buy you a farm eh dad?

RAFIQUE: I would be happy if you would get a job poothar.

TARIQ: Actually...I've been looking. You ask Uncle Abdul or Majid. I went down the job centre today... It's all crap.

DEEMA: Yeah, well you gotta start somewhere haven't ya?

RAFIQUE finishes eating and pours himself a glass of water, drinks it and sets it down.

RAFIQUE: I have work for you. You can take them to Coventry for me.

TARIQ: You what?

RAFIQUE: Five gone already.

DEEMA: Maybe you should try and give them back.

RAFIQUE: Tariq?

DEEMA: Give me the number. I'll talk to Mr Dickson.

RAFIQUE: I can look after my own affairs.

DEEMA: I'll explain things to him. See if we can work somethin' out.

RAFIQUE: It is in hand poothar... Tariq?

TARIQ: Sorry dad... can't...gotta small job on.

RAFIQUE: Then do one more small job son.

TARIQ: I would but it's too late to sort it out… I promised a mate…he's waitin' for me.

RAFIQUE: Do mates put a roof over your head?

TARIQ: Maybe in a couple of days…I'll see what I can do yeah?

RAFIQUE: Mahmood will take them. I can only try. That is all. The rest is my good luck.

TARIQ: I'll see what I can do dad.

ZAINAB gets up.

ZAINAB: (*To TARIQ.*) Come Tariq.

ZAINAB points to a box .

Lift it… Put by the wall.

TARIQ attempts to move the box but can't manage it.

TARIQ: Legs are hurtin' mom…I'll help you tomorra…

ZAINAB: How can you help me poothar?

RAFIQUE: You carry yourself in defeat… Look at you. Skin is hanging off your bones. My arm is fatter than your leg. At your age we had the bodies of statues and the spirits of warriors.

TARIQ: I'm alright.

ZAINAB: How many weeks I didn't see your face?

TARIQ: I had things to do.

ZAINAB: Things you are doing I know.

DEEMA: He's here now umee.

ZAINAB: Kill yourself if you like. I will not cry any more.

TARIQ: I don't want you to.

RAFIQUE: What have you become poothar? A walking corpse. A father should not have to bury his son.

TARIQ: I'll be alright.

RAFIQUE: The shame has half killed me. You will do the rest.

DEEMA: Dad…you finished eating?

DEEMA starts to clear away the rest of the dishes.

ZAINAB picks up her plant and waters it with some water from her glass.

ZAINAB: My Rani needs light. I will set her by the sink. The sun is stronger there. (*ZAINAB sets it down in a sunnier spot.*) So warm inside…Aunty Sara is growing hers very big…when I make the greenhouse…I will ask Jamil. Such a blessing…a child who knows his duty…who stands before he is asked…a smart child.

TARIQ: Ain't got a GCSE to his name. He couldn't even spell 'business studies'.

RAFIQUE: It is actions that count. He runs his father's business dausth.

TARIQ: I know that.

RAFIQUE: He has a legitimate concern.

TARIQ: You 'avin' a laugh?

DEEMA: This is not funny Tariq.

ZAINAB: Children who grieve their parents will never succeed in life. It will be many years gone when you realise.

DEEMA: It's no one's fault umee. It's not our fault.

TARIQ: Don't you wish you could leg it sometimes… Same old down-on-you attitude…actin' as if the world's gonna end tomorrow… Don't you get scared that you're gonna end up livin' and dyin' in this little area…know what I mean dad?

RAFIQUE: I have lived and travelled and inshallah I will many more times.

TARIQ: You have? Where you been then?

DEEMA: Shut up Tariq.

RAFIQUE: And where have you Valayithee educated British been to? You…you have managed to drive to Telford…that is your achievement.

TARIQ: I'm still young.

RAFIQUE: And yet…some people…they are like bulldogs, full of strength, determination, fire.

TARIQ: D'you know what? Stick to Mahmood and his wonderful son Jamil. You're right. They've got it sussed.

ZAINAB: Uncle Mahmood.

DEEMA: This isn't why you came.

TARIQ: Gimme a break sis…what did I come here for eh? What was I thinking?

RAFIQUE: I didn't ask you.

TARIQ: Least I don't have any regrets.

RAFIQUE: How do you regret nothing?

TARIQ: I don't know dad. Maybe you could fill me in.

DEEMA: What are you carrying on for?

TARIQ: He's the expert man. He can tell me what he thinks about his life…what he's made of it… How old are you now…fifty and then some? So what d'you have to be proud of? Tellin' us all how wonderful you are and how you've suffered. What did you give us? What did I 'ave?

RAFIQUE: Why did we bother?

TARIQ: You tell me. We didn't make you come here. I didn't ask to be born.

RAFIQUE stands up affronted and grabs TARIQ by the back of the neck almost forcing his head into the bowl of chicken curry.

ZAINAB: Stop…Bhaas!

ZAINAB frees TARIQ from RAFIQUE's grip.

RAFIQUE: See that chicken…I have to beg you to leave the house for the ten-yard walk to the butcher's so you can bring it for your mother to cook and feed you… We had to chase them round the yard and kill them ourselves if we wanted to eat. We walked six miles a day to school, did our schoolwork or got the soti [stick]. Most days, roti was onions and yoghurt and we were happy with that. You leave the land you love so one day your children will stand. Higher than you ever dreamed, touching the sky…and all you get back are insults and a broken heart.

Beat.

ZAINAB: We came because they let us…we came because it was a place to try…to not be hungry.

DEEMA: We know umee.

RAFIQUE: You do not know. Nothing.

Beat.

TARIQ: Jimmy's a tosser…he just plays up to you and you fall for it.

DEEMA: Tariq.

ZAINAB: He has never been tosser to me.

RAFIQUE: Deema…don't follow this one. You are sensible.

DEEMA: I'm not followin' anyone.

TARIQ: Forget it man. He don't see nothing. He's blind.

RAFIQUE: I can see perfect.

TARIQ: Whoever sold you them books took you for a right mug din't they?

DEEMA: Shut it.

RAFIQUE: I am mug?

TARIQ: You've gotta admit it.

DEEMA: Pack it in.

RAFIQUE: Me…a mug. You load of shit!

Offstage, there is banging on the front door, but it is not heard in all the shouting.

TARIQ: You load of shit!

ZAINAB: You all are shit to me.

DEEMA: Umee.

Banging continues. They hear it for the first time. They all stop.

RAFIQUE: There is someone. Go to the door.

DEEMA exits.

ZAINAB: We should have beaten you when you were small.

RAFIQUE: Just like those ghaureh [whites] they will have nobody. What is family to them?

ZAINAB: A burden to be rid of…a curse to be free from.

DEEMA re-enters panicked.

DEEMA: Tariq! They're outside!

ZAINAB: Who is outside?

Banging starts again. ZAINAB gets up.

DEEMA: Mom, don't.

RAFIQUE: Who is it…?

TARIQ: Dunno…

DEEMA: Tariq.

RAFIQUE: You bring your painchaud druggie friends here, breaking the door?

TARIQ: No…I…I…don't know who it is.

Banging continues as TARIQ makes to run out. RAFIQUE holds him back.

DEEMA: It's Jimmy. He sent them.

RAFIQUE: Are you paaghal? [crazy]

TARIQ: He's a drug-dealer dad. Imports it…

ZAINAB: Jamil?

TARIQ: He is…he… I work fer him…he gives me gear. It's true.

RAFIQUE: Shut up…shut up!

TARIQ: I din't do nothin' dad…I swear.

RAFIQUE: With what face do I call you mine?

RAFIQUE lets go of TARIQ.

Call the police…Deema.

More banging as DEEMA fumbles for her phone and TARIQ makes to run out the back exit of the house. DEEMA drops her phone.

DEEMA: Don't go outside!

TARIQ: I have to.

TARIQ exits as ZAINAB takes her chappal off and waves it in her hand.

ZAINAB: I will show you now…fuckun bhaastur buchey! [fucking bastard children]

RAFIQUE: Wait, Zainab.

ZAINAB rushes to the door and RAFIQUE chase after her.

Get away… We called the police!

ZAINAB: Get out from my house!

Shouting and a scuffle is overheard followed by ZAINAB's shouting, a thud and a scream…

DEEMA: Dad!

Lights down.

Act Two

A darkened inner-city street. Early hours, the next morning. JIMMY is standing over TARIQ who is lying beaten and bloody at his feet.

JIMMY: You are such a pune ain't ya?

JIMMY pulls TARIQ up by his jacket and he sets him against a wall.

Why would you wanna be so stupid…I just don't understand man.

TARIQ: I ain't done nothin' Jim.

JIMMY: It's one thing some prick holdin' you up and skanking ya. That's the enemy you know, get it? The sort you can look up another day… But after all I did for you and you try a sneaky one like that. I have to show you.

TARIQ: I came to see ya.

JIMMY punches TARIQ on his bloody face and TARIQ screams out in pain.

JIMMY: Suddenly got a conscience did ya?

TARIQ: They din't do nothin'…my family Din't do nothing.

JIMMY: And what have I ever done to them Taz? What have I ever done to you eh? Bailed you out whenever some fucker tried to batter you at school. Good few had a go din't they? But every time cousing Jimmy dealt with it. Didn't he? Didn't he?

TARIQ: Yeah Jimmy.

JIMMY: I let you work fer me…cos you were family.

TARIQ: Jimmy, I ain't got any money.

JIMMY puts his arm round TARIQ and hugs him close, mocking affection.

JIMMY: (*Laughing.*) I ain't poor or nothin'…I make that money in a couple of days. But you have pulled my pants down in public… Even the lowlifes on the corners are callin' me a pussy. What d'you wanna do now? Bend me over and fuck me up the arse? I'm Jamil Mahmood right… I have a name. You get my name back or your tongue will taste my shit proper. Okay?

TARIQ: Kusmeh Jimmy, you've gotta believe me.

JIMMY: What did you say?

TARIQ: I didn't do it.

JIMMY: No, just now, Kusmeh.

TARIQ: Kusmeh.

JIMMY: That's it… D'you know what a kusum is?

TARIQ: I swear.

JIMMY: That is serious Tariq. You're swearing on God's name. Say 'Quran Nee Kusmeh'.

TARIQ: Quran Nee Kusmeh.

JIMMY: Now you're swearing on the Holy Book… Say kusmeh on your mother's life.

TARIQ: I swear…kusmeh…on my mom's life.

JIMMY punches him again.

JIMMY: See, you little… Now if anything happens to your mom. It'll be your fault. That's what I hated about you lot the most…no fear of the Almighty. Too much of this place has got to your head. How many times did I say…use the place man…you're in England. Make some pounds…set yourself up but never forget…don't try to be a white man. You're such a kaafur… I don't blame ya you know…if my old man was about to lose his house or get banged up, I'd have to try an' 'elp him as well… Maybe if you'd asked me, maybe…bein' family, I could help…but then again, never trust a junkie eh?

TARIQ: Okay, okay, I thought about it but I didn't. I couldn't.

JIMMY: Listen to me…what's done is done…you've got until Jum'aa. I'll be at the big mosque…I'll be out after namaaz. (*Beat.*) Don't come in cos you're pleeth. [unclean]

TARIQ: Where am I gonna find that sort of money?

JIMMY: I don't care who you have to get it from, your mom, your daadee or shit it out.

TARIQ's legs buckle and JIMMY grabs him.

You'll be okay… A man has to grow up some day, can't hide behind mummy and daddy forever can ya?

TARIQ: No.

JIMMY: How are they your family?

TARIQ: Alright.

JIMMY: Yeah well, best not to get the pigs involved isn't it brother?

TARIQ: No Jimmy.

JIMMY: You what?

TARIQ: Yeah Jimmy.

Beat.

JIMMY: D'you wan' a lift?

JIMMY grabs TARIQ by the arm and walks away. Fade out.

SCENE TWO

Early morning, the next day. Indoors. Through the window, neat rows of plants in the garden. The Raath Kee Rani plant is in a large pot in a corner with plastic surrounding it. TARIQ is on the sofa. His jacket has been flung in a corner. DEEMA is dabbing TCP on his eye with cotton wool.

DEEMA: What did you tell mum?

TARIQ: (*Laughs.*) Got into a fight with a pissed-up skinhead…

DEEMA: It ain't funny Tariq… What about dad?

TARIQ: I just walked in man.

DEEMA: Sit still.

TARIQ: Just leave it…it's stingin' like a…aaow…

DEEMA stops dabbing, lights a cigarette and starts again.

DEEMA: The police wanna speak to ya.

TARIQ: What d'you call them for?

DEEMA: There were men trying to break into the house. They broke the front door.

TARIQ: I'll get it fixed alright.

DEEMA: If you don't go and see them I will. I'll tell 'em all about your deals with Jimmy.

TARIQ: Don't be stupid…

DEEMA: Stupid? This is stupid Tariq… You are stupid.

TARIQ: D'you think it'll all be okay if we go to the cops. D'you think Jimmy can't get me back?

DEEMA: You took it…you took his money…

TARIQ: Just leave it Deema… I din't take it okay.

DEEMA: You idiot.

TARIQ: He's got away with pushin' me around for too long.

DEEMA: You think Jimmy's gonna respect you now. He laughs at you.

TARIQ: Well…he ain't laughing now…

DEEMA: I thought you were starting to think straight… I thought you'd finally got some sense… I don't buy it.

TARIQ: You'll just have to. I said I didn't take it okay… / Shhh! She's coming.

DEEMA: This isn't…

DEEMA panics and tries to pass the cigarette to TARIQ but drops it. ZAINAB enters as TARIQ is picking it up laughing. ZAINAB walks a little slowly, as if in pain. She carries a prescription. DEEMA tries to resume cleaning TARIQ's face but ZAINAB takes the cotton wool from her and starts rubbing his face with it.

ZAINAB: A face like a pig is funny?

TARIQ: No mom.

ZAINAB: Your father has a headache. Stop making noise.

TARIQ: Is he alright?

ZAINAB hands the prescription to DEEMA.

ZAINAB: Deema…get my tablets from chemist.

TARIQ: I'll go check on dad.

ZAINAB: You keep away from the room or you will have one more on the other side.

TARIQ: How's your back?

Beat.

ZAINAB: Hurting.

DEEMA: We should go to the doctor again.

ZAINAB: A bruise, that is all.

DEEMA: He fell on you umee.

ZAINAB: Did you see his arm? Lucky I was there… Those koothey [dogs] will not come here again.

TARIQ: I'm sorry umee jee…

ZAINAB: They will not come here again Tariq.

TARIQ: No mom…gonna put my head down okay?

TARIQ exits leaving his jacket. Beat.

DEEMA: Your plant's grown nice.

ZAINAB: The dirt is good. If you feed it, it will make you happy. If you love something, it loves you back.

DEEMA: Not really.

ZAINAB: In its own way.

DEEMA: You can give for years and get nothing back… Look at dad.

ZAINAB: That is different. A man is a man, they are all the same. Many people in the family will be happy to marry you.

DEEMA: Maybe I don't want to, maybe I have a plan.

ZAINAB: Another big talker you are. I have known many of them.

DEEMA: I mean it.

ZAINAB: Do you know…I was the most spoilt child in my family. Every day, I would run to Beji's [granny's] house and she would feed me mukainee roti with so much butter. Your aunty help Beji cook and clean and I would swim in the dam with my friends, catch fish and bring them home. Beji…she shouts at me, pull my plait and drag me to the choolaa [fire] and tell me: 'Stir choorail, learn what is important,' (*Laughs.*) but I never did…I learnt when I came here.

DEEMA: It doesn't work that way now. You don't have to live in a cage. Dad and Tariq, they're big men

ZAINAB: Your father. It is for me to look after him.

DEEMA: Who looks after you mom?

ZAINAB: I don't need. Nothing…thank you.

DEEMA: I used to watch dad when he came in after a day out cruising the Peak District or touring with friends. Soon as he was through the door, you'd be there with tea, roti. I'd watch him lie down on the sofa, put his legs up onto your lap and you would press them for hours.

ZAINAB: You do not know.

DEEMA: Get the bowl, heat the water, pour the salt, carry it in, wash his feet. I'd watch his face and all I saw was nothing. It was like he didn't see you. Like he didn't see any of us, like he'd do anything to swap places with the man at the Peak District. It was as if he was saying, 'Look what you've done to me,' and you were silent. He was silent. It was all nothing.

ZAINAB: He had dreams to make more.

DEEMA: And I used to think, what sort of man would cause so much misery to a woman like you.

ZAINAB: He had many grand schemes.

DEEMA: I used to say my duahs at night so that God would come and teach him what it is to be a husband, a father.

ZAINAB: Your father has been a friend to many… A wife has to look after her partner.

DEEMA: Partner? He's never even poured you a glass of water from the kitchen tap.

ZAINAB: From child to old man, so many dreams for us all…dreams that even the Ottomans in a thousand lifetimes could not fulfil. In thirty years he never touched me. He always tried to make a better life. Some people's souls are too soft Deema. They are not tough enough for this world.

DEEMA: While he was dreaming, you worked, don't you understand that? You could have done…

ZAINAB: And if we do as they do where are we all?

DEEMA: Not as they do.

ZAINAB: A waste of time my dear…a waste of years…a waste
of hopes… Be sensible…settle down…it will be right.
There is Tariq to think of…what will happen to him? I am
your mother. You know I will see what is best for you.

ZAINAB gets up to exit.

DEEMA: Umee

ZAINAB stops.

It's nothing.

*ZAINAB exits. DEEMA fishes into TARIQ's jacket pockets, looking
for money. She pulls out a screwdriver. She exits.*

Lights down.

SCENE THREE

*Later the same day. JIMMY enters KERRY's flat with DEEMA. He is
carrying a shopping bag containing two cans of fizzy drink.*

JIMMY: Can't work it out.

DEEMA: What?

*There is a carrier bag on the floor next to the table. He goes over
to it and sits down, opens the shopping bag and passes DEEMA
a can. She takes it and sits down opposite him, opens her can
and has a drink.*

JIMMY: Why you stuck around here.

DEEMA: Why'd you stick around?

*JIMMY takes a remote control device and aims it at the music
player. An Asian Hip-Hop fusion track kicks in. He starts to
count money from the other bag and stacks it up into a neat pile
on the table.*

JIMMY: This is where it all is, where I belong.

DEEMA: Where you can be the boss?

JIMMY: Same biddies behind the counters, same cousins around the corner, same scum kickin' about in the gutter, it kind of makes you feel secure…appreciated.

DEEMA: Didn't know you had a fan club.

JIMMY: Your dad's keeping it going all by himself.

DEEMA: He's a good judge of character my dad.

JIMMY: That's why you lot get slagged off. None of you wanna follow the rules. You all wanna be different. Rafique? He's dreamin' about bein' a king in mansions he couldn't even be a cleaner in. Tariq lives for brown an' you… (*Laughs.*) …you think you can be more of a bloke than me.

DEEMA puts her can onto the table and stands up.

DEEMA: It doesn't take much.

JIMMY: You what?

DEEMA: To be more of a bloke than you.

JIMMY: Full of smart words and uppity chat. You really impress me.

DEEMA: Jimmy…will you leave my brother alone?

JIMMY: Knew it.

DEEMA: I'm asking.

JIMMY: Only a true coward who sends his little sister round to beg for him.

DEEMA: He didn't and I'm not.

JIMMY: So why you here?

DEEMA: You beat him up.

JIMMY: I wouldn't do that Deem.

DEEMA: And the thugs you sent to the house… You…you made your point alright.

JIMMY: What did he tell ya?

DEEMA: You beat him up Jimmy.

JIMMY: I found him on the street looking like shit so I dropped him at your mom's. An' what thugs… We're cousins man. What's he tellin' stories for? He must've been concussed.

DEEMA: I'll get your money.

JIMMY: How you gonna do that?

DEEMA: I'm going full-time at the shop. Nine grand isn't it… Take a few months but I will do it… So can it stop?

JIMMY: You're a shop assistant. I've got a heart.

DEEMA: Alright…I'll get a loan…I'll go to the bank.

JIMMY: Another Chaudhry debt… I can see them rollin' out the red carpet for you down the Barclays.

DEEMA: I will.

JIMMY: Wouldn't put you in that situation.

DEEMA: I don't ask you for anything Jimmy…just this once… please.

JIMMY: You don't have to.

JIMMY stands up and walks over to DEEMA, eventually being beside her.

DEEMA: I mean it.

JIMMY: Come away with me.

DEEMA: I will pay you back.

JIMMY: What about Pakistan? We could stay at The Pearl Continental, take a tour of Murree…get some business done, it's a growing market out there.

DEEMA: Is this a joke?

JIMMY: I was gonna take my dad but we could take this one step further.

DEEMA: You're off your head.

JIMMY: Course not.

DEEMA: Me go to Pakistan with you?

JIMMY: It's where we're from…our homeland… Think about it.

DEEMA: C'mon Jimmy.

JIMMY: Maybe Tariq doesn't have to pay me back.

DEEMA: It has to finish.

JIMMY: You were right to come here.

JIMMY moves closer to DEEMA and she moves back.

DEEMA: We used to feel sorry for you…me and Tariq.

JIMMY stops.

Remember when you wagged school and sat in next door's garden, up their tree, smoking a fag. Your dad came chargin' up the path, yanked you off and started punching you in the head…again and again.

JIMMY: Don't be silly.

DEEMA: Mum was screamin', beggin' him to stop but he didn't. He wouldn't.

JIMMY tries to grab her but she pulls away and he laughs. KERRY wakes from within and watches.

Never seen a man in such a state… Thought you were gonna die.

JIMMY: It didn't happen like that.

DEEMA: What were you? Twelve…thirteen? You just stood there…didn't even move…didn't make a sound.

JIMMY: Now you're makin' a drama out of it… You shou'n't try and think too much…messes up your pretty head.

JIMMY tries to kiss DEEMA. She stops him.

Why d'you come here all on your own? Don't get me wrong…this is what I want. This is what our parents want…it keeps us all together. We're blood and we should stick together.

DEEMA: You're high.

JIMMY: Don't say you haven't thought about it.

JIMMY picks up the envelope and throws it at DEEMA.

Open it… Just have a look.

DEEMA opens up the envelope and finds two tickets in it.

Two tickets to Islamabad. Rafique is up fer it, believe me.

DEEMA: You seriously think I'm gonna catch a plane…

JIMMY: He told my dad it'd be the happiest day for him…his daughter married to a boy with such good prospects and a family union.

DEEMA: He wouldn't…

JIMMY: He did say let's wait and see…but what does he know eh?

JIMMY is slowly trying to take her top off but DEEMA backs away, falling onto the sofa.

DEEMA: He would never…

JIMMY: I'd look after him…Tariq…he ain't that bad Deem. I've always had a soft spot for him… Maybe he could run one of the shops if he gets himself ship-shape. Maybe he could run one of your shops.

DEEMA: Mine?

JIMMY: Course. My wife's gonna own her own place… Your family could rest easy… They're all game for it.

DEEMA: This ain't a drug deal… I'm not a kilo of gear…

JIMMY: Oh no…no. You are your own woman and you ain't no sniveller… 'S why you get to me…we'd be husband and wife. Give me a chance.

DEEMA: But Kerry?

JIMMY: She's out. A means to an end.

DEEMA: She know that?

JIMMY: Women like her are scavengers, beggin' round the streets for the scraps. An arrangement Deem. (*Laughing.*) She's not special. She's not pure…

As he kisses her chest, DEEMA recoils.

C'mon…you're not that shy.

DEEMA grabs the screwdriver and plunges it into the top of his leg. JIMMY screams as DEEMA stands up and KERRY enters.

Aaaeh…what did you do that for? You…crazy bitch.

DEEMA: Come near me and I'll fucken do it again.

JIMMY: I'm bleedin'!

KERRY: Oh yeah you are.

JIMMY: Kes…what are you…? See what she did? You…you were out.

KERRY: Just as well dad said he was going bingo babe ain't it?

JIMMY: Don't stand there.

KERRY: (*To DEEMA.*) What is it with you lot? Do you have to fuck everyone you're related to?

DEEMA: I didn't.

JIMMY: She attacked me!

KERRY: Undress you with her fists did she?

JIMMY: She went for me, I swear babe.

KERRY: Snoopin' around pretendin' to look for your brother were ya?

DEEMA: I came to talk.

KERRY: What did he give ya? You should've got somethin' babe… Every time I kiss Jimmy he passes me a wrap… quite romantic really.

DEEMA: Rather be dead in a ditch than touch him…no offence.

JIMMY is attempting to move but KERRY pushes him down and he yelps.

JIMMY: Aaargh!

KERRY: Don't talk Jimmy. (*KERRY goes to the table and looks at the money. She picks up the tickets.*) British Airways…aah… were you gonna surprise me baby?

JIMMY: Yeah…she…she tried to rob me.

DEEMA: Said I had to go with him. He said women like you are a means to an end.

JIMMY: Lying bitch.

DEEMA starts to straighten her clothes.

DEEMA: Don't come near my family again.

JIMMY: Or what slag?

KERRY: Dunno why you din't finish him off. In my opinion, if you 'ave to hurt a person to make a point then do it properly…do some damage.

DEEMA: He's your boyfriend.

KERRY: Yeah he is ain't he?

DEEMA: Good luck.

DEEMA picks up the screwdriver and puts it in her jacket. She makes to leave.

JIMMY: What you doin'? Stop her!

DEEMA exits.

What you do that for?

Beat. KERRY goes to the money on the table and picks it up. JIMMY watches her.

Call a taxi fer us.

Beat.

KERRY: You said it was me an' you.

JIMMY: It is.

KERRY: You said your family would take to me.

JIMMY: I'm working on it.

KERRY: (*Laughs.*) I've been hoping for ages.

JIMMY: Fuck's sake, Kerry, I need to get to the hospital.

KERRY: What was I to you Jimmy?

JIMMY: Eh?

KERRY: What am I to you?

JIMMY: Please…I'm fainting.

KERRY: (*Looking through the money.*) Tariq was right.

JIMMY: That cunt is dead.

KERRY: C'mon Jimmy. You don't wanna see me up in court against ya.

JIMMY tries to stand up, dragging his leg. KERRY picks up the tickets.

Ooh first claaas…we are royalty ain't we?

KERRY rips up the tickets.

JIMMY: Don't do that…they cost grands.

KERRY throws them at JIMMY.

KERRY: I was watching…don't you get it?

JIMMY: Babe. That din't mean nothin'…you have to to keep people happy. It's expected.

KERRY: An arrangement? How sad. Those poor bitches don't know what's comin' do they?

JIMMY hobbles up.

JIMMY: You're still my one Kez.

KERRY pushes him onto the floor again.

Oww!

KERRY: You never looked at me Jimmy.

JIMMY: I look at you all the time.

KERRY: not properly…not with heart…not…not like you felt me.

Beat.

JIMMY: C'mon Kez.

KERRY packs the cash into a bag and comes in and out grabbing clothing and shoving it into a bag.

What…what you doin'?

KERRY: Cleanin' up.

JIMMY: That's my money…that's mine.

KERRY: Want your money do ya? Well, it's gone, okay. Think Tariq took the nine grand? He can't even rob a newsagent's properly. It was me alright. I had it all the time.

JIMMY: You didn't.

KERRY: Was keeping it safe…kind of insurance really…but now I think about it…good thing I held onto it. All these years I've been keeping your arse cos you're too stingy and mommy-lovin' to get us a place. (*KERRY picks up the bag.*) So if you want it come and find me. Reckon it's the least you can do for me, don't you?

JIMMY: Alright…you've had your fun… I'm…I'm sorry alright.

KERRY walks up to JIMMY and gets up close in his face.

KERRY: Wrong Jimmy darling…I'm just starting. I was thinkin' of seein' Majorca…or Tenerife. Our mum used to say it was gorgeous out there…hot sand, bright sun and the people are lovely. Just the right time o' year as well…or maybe Ibiza… Splash out, why not…what do I care…? Got plenty of time me… Maybe I'll find myself a suave, Spanish geezer…bit of class… No offence Jimmy but you din't get me goin'…know what I mean…

JIMMY: I dragged you out of shit, you bitch.

KERRY: You kept me in it. (*Beat.*) If you ask me you were lucky…I would've stabbed you right there.

Punches him in the chest and throws him the phone.

Best call Ubaa [dad] before the cops get here.

JIMMY: Kerry…

KERRY leaves.

Come back…you fucken rundee! [whore]

Lights down.

SCENE FOUR

The garden at the Chaudhry's house. A week later. It is afternoon. There is a fire in the tandoor. RAFIQUE is sitting on the bench with his feet up reading a magazine supplement. His right forearm is bandaged up. There are particulars of country estates lying about and a copy of 'The Field' magazine on the bench. There are boxes of books lined up near the tandoor. TARIQ is sitting on the edge of the tandoor, drinking a glass of milk. ZAINAB is examining her Raath Kee Rani plant.

ZAINAB: She's dying

TARIQ: You should be in bed dad.

RAFIQUE: I said so.

TARIQ: A glass of milk and lots of sleep…'s wat you need, trust me.

ZAINAB: My Raath kee Rani.

RAFIQUE: Didn't I say so?

TARIQ picks up a stray cookery book and hands it to his mother.

TARIQ: Missed one.

ZAINAB throws the book into the fire.

ZAINAB: Go get more…

TARIQ looks at RAFIQUE.

TARIQ: Mom?

ZAINAB: Hurry up…next to television.

TARIQ exits.

RAFIQUE: It is not the result…it is the effort we make that matters.

ZAINAB: I don't understand.

RAFIQUE: These are delicate plants. This is not a delicate climate.

ZAINAB: They are selling lemon trees at Asda. After court you can bring one for me in Saeed's car.

RAFIQUE: I have a meeting with Mr Dickson.

ZAINAB: Ten minutes it will take.

RAFIQUE: Lemon trees grow in hot countries.

ZAINAB: Bring it…if they take the house I will have my plants at least.

RAFIQUE: Stupid woman… You talk of things you don't understand… You don't listen. We are keeping it I am saying…the court will decide the monthlies. That is all. This is my house. It will always be my house.

ZAINAB: Paid for with Mahmood's money…clever man.

RAFIQUE: And I will pay him back. I have a plan.

ZAINAB: You do?

RAFIQUE: You think I have run out of ideas?

ZAINAB reaches into the top of her kameez, takes out a five pound note and holds it out for RAFIQUE.

ZAINAB: Bring the tree. You can do that for me.

RAFIQUE takes the note. Enter DEEMA. She is wearing a black knee-length skirt with thick woollen tights, a blouse and a jumper to match the skirt. She carries a hairbrush and a hairband. She hands the hairbrush and band to ZAINAB who begins to fashion her hair into a ponytail.

RAFIQUE: Where are your clothes?

DEEMA: I'm wearing them.

RAFIQUE: Put some trousers with this… tell her.

ZAINAB finishes the tight ponytail and hands the hairbrush back to DEEMA.

ZAINAB: I will sew some trousers.

DEEMA: I'm not gettin' changed okay. It's comfortable.

RAFIQUE: Where are my gauliyaah? [tablets] (*Beat.*) Zainab?

ZAINAB: In the cupboard next to the fridge.

RAFIQUE gets up to exit and trips over a holdall in the door way.

RAFIQUE: I don't know where to look in this house. (*RAFIQUE brings the holdall in with his good left arm.*) Why must you people leave junk everywhere?

DEEMA: It's not junk. It's mine.

ZAINAB: So much things?

DEEMA: The training's in Earl's Court… London.

RAFIQUE: Who will help your mother with the roti?

DEEMA: You'll have to help her.

RAFIQUE: I am going to cook…in my position?

ZAINAB: What did I do to push you all away? They will say it was my fault

DEEMA: They always say something. They don't matter.

RAFIQUE: You cannot say your family 'don't matter'. (*Beat. Blows his nose.*) my tablets Zainab.

ZAINAB exits. DEEMA puts her hairbrush into her holdall.

All the problems are gone and you are going? It is all getting better…

DEEMA: What about today dad?

RAFIQUE: Today…today we all are here. So the books did not sell. Khan Sahib is not wanting payment. I can try again. Six months from now…

DEEMA: I thought I was the one going mad. You and your stories.

RAFIQUE: What are you talking?

DEEMA: Tomorrow we'll be rich…too rich. Today we have no school clothes, bus fare, food… Stories.

RAFIQUE: Success does not come with the click of a finger marri thee. [my daughter] Mistakes are made but you must have patience…face the hard times…not run away.

DEEMA: Is it so hard for you to just get on…to just do something?

RAFIQUE: What real wealth in this dooniya [world] my child? The reason to try, the reason to fight.

DEEMA: I bet you couldn't change a light bulb in this house. She even has to do that for you.

RAFIQUE: Of course I… Have you hurt your head?

DEEMA: For once in your life stop living in your head and see what's really there. Look at us. You made decisions. Me, mum, Tariq, this house. This is where you have been. This is where you are…what you have done. Are you blind?

Beat.

RAFIQUE: I have not helped you. I cannot help Tariq.

DEEMA sits and puts her bags down.

DEEMA: I'm sorry. I didn't mean.

RAFIQUE: Time is going. I must put on my suit.

ZAINAB re-enters with RAFIQUE's tablets and a glass of water. ZAINAB offers him the tablets but he doesn't respond so she puts them down.

DEEMA: I'm still here dad.

RAFIQUE gets up, places his hand on his daughter's head.

RAFIQUE: You are a good daughter. I knew you would be.

RAFIQUE exits and DEEMA looks down at her feet.

ZAINAB: That is fine. I have no work but to chase his tail. Where is your brother?

DEEMA: He went inside.

ZAINAB: And he has fallen into a box I think. Hurry up and bring me the books before the fire burns out. (*ZAINAB stokes the fire and picks up odd pieces of paper to throw into it.*) And when you get back you can help me sort the house. Have you seen the upstairs? I cannot do it on my own. I only have two hands.

DEEMA: Get them to do it.

ZAINAB: (*Laughs.*) What have they ever done? I will paint the hallway…but first we have to scrape off the old paper. Have you seen it? What a mess.

TARIQ re-enters without any books. He sees the fire and remembers what he was asked.

TARIQ: Oh sh…I needed the toilet umee… Anyway dunno which ones you mean… Give us a hand Deem.

DEEMA stands up. Beat.

DEEMA: Don't wait for me mom.

ZAINAB: I have no time for waiting.

TARIQ crouches down by the soil and messes with the plants as if distracted. DEEMA goes to ZAINAB who is standing by the fire looking in. DEEMA touches her. At first ZAINAB does not react. Then she turns to face her.

Find your own way.

DEEMA: I will.

DEEMA goes to hug ZAINAB but ZAINAB will not.

ZAINAB: I must take tablets to your father.

ZAINAB grabs the tablets and exits. DEEMA buttons up her jacket. TARIQ is scraping a small garden fork on the ground.

TARIQ: Now you've gone and upset her. Should give people a bit of notice shou'n't ya? Instead of just goin' off like that.

DEEMA: Shut up Tariq.

TARIQ: What you bein' funny for?

DEEMA: You do it all the time.

TARIQ: Not deliberately…I mean I try not to…sometimes… (*Beat.*) What about Jimmy? What if he finds you before the cops get him?

DEEMA: He can't do anything.

TARIQ: Me and Kerry…

DEEMA: What d'you mean you and Kerry?

TARIQ: She's alright Deem….we went down to the clinic in Stechford…just opened, s'posed to be the business this one. They said I've got a good chance of gettin' a place to detox and that… We're gonna do it. I'll be a different person when you come back.

DEEMA: I'm not comin' back.

TARIQ: After yer trainin' I mean.

DEEMA: They're gonna help me find a flat.

TARIQ: What about mum an' dad?

DEEMA: I'll phone 'em.

Beat.

TARIQ: You're just gonna go?

DEEMA: The woman was really nice…said there's room for promotion.

TARIQ: Serious Deema.

DEEMA: I'll be flyin' out after a couple of months.

TARIQ: I wanna clean up… Don't you believe me? I wanna make a go of it… I can see myself workin'…a real job with payslips an' all… It's about time…get myself proper sorted.

DEEMA: That's good. I'm glad.

Beat.

TARIQ: You can't fucken leave me at home with these two.

DEEMA: So get out.

TARIQ: I'm gonna… What am I supposed to say to them?

DEEMA: Say what you like.

TARIQ: That should work.

Beat.

DEEMA: D'you know what it feels like. I can't watch it any more. Every time I look at you, it's like someone's stuck a knife in my guts, they're twistin' it all round and they just won't stop. Every time dad an' mum…that knife digs in a bit more and it's like the blood is filling up in my lungs until it's in my throat and I'm suffocating…I'm suffocating.

TARIQ: It ain't easy gettin' off this shit.

DEEMA: I am ready to breathe again.

TARIQ stands up to face his sister.

TARIQ: I just need you to believe in me.

DEEMA: I have. I do.

TARIQ: I know…but it's time Deema.

DEEMA: It is. Believe in yourself Tariq.

Beat.

TARIQ: C'mon sis. You're alright. We're alright ain't we?

DEEMA: Course we are.

TARIQ: See you down there…before you know it…yeah?

DEEMA: Yeah.

DEEMA carries her holdall and exits. TARIQ sits staring at the garden. He goes over to where the Raath kee Rani plant is and starts to dig it out with the fork slowly. He throws the fork down and starts to dig with his hands. He throws the plant to one side.

As the soil piles up, he reaches under and pulls out a small plastic bag, the size of a small sweetie bag, containing heroin. He dusts it down and puts it into his pocket. He exits.

End.